# *Life After Death*
## A Legal and Practical Guide
## for Surviving Spouses

Marilyn W. McWilliams
Moye White LLP
1400 16th Street, 6th Floor
Denver, CO 80202

BRADFORD PUBLISHING CO.
Denver, Colorado

# DISCLAIMER

This book is intended to provide general information with regard to the subject matter covered. It is not meant to provide legal opinions or to offer advice, nor to serve as a substitute for advice by licensed, legal or other professionals. This book is sold with the understanding that Bradford Publishing Company and the author(s), by virtue of its publication, are not engaged in rendering legal or other professional services to the reader.

Bradford Publishing Company and the author(s) do not warrant that the information contained in this book is complete or accurate, and do not assume and hereby disclaim any liability to any person for any loss or damage caused by errors, inaccuracies or omissions, or usage of this book. Third-party products mentioned herein are for examples only and do not constitute either an endorsement or recommendation. No party connected with this publication assumes any responsibility concerning the selection or performance as a result of their use.

Laws, and interpretations of those laws, change frequently, and the subject matter of this book can have important legal consequences that may vary from one individual to the next. It is therefore the responsibility of the reader to know whether, and to what extent, this information is applicable to his or her situation, and if necessary, to consult legal, tax, or other counsel.

## *Library of Congress Cataloging-in-Publication Data*

McWilliams, Marilyn W.
  Life after death : a legal and practical guide for surviving spouses /
Marilyn W. McWilliams.
      p. cm.
  ISBN 1-932779-12-4
  1. Widows--United States--Life skills guides. 2. Widowers--United
States--Life skills guides. 3. Widows--Legal status, laws, etc.--United
States. 4. Widowers--Legal status, laws, etc.--United States. I. Title.

  HQ1058.5.U5M36 2005
  306.88'3'0973--dc22

                                    2005020864

*Life After Death: A Legal and Practical Guide for Surviving Spouses*
ISBN: 1-932779-12-4

Published 2005 by Bradford Publishing Company
1743 Wazee Street, Denver, Colorado 80202
www.bradfordpublishing.com

# ABOUT THE AUTHOR

Concentrating primarily on estate planning and administration for estates of all sizes, Marilyn McWilliams advises individuals, families, and closely-held businesses in this complex arena. From creating revocable and irrevocable trusts, charitable trusts, residence trusts, and advising fiduciaries and trustees to acting as a trust administrator and incorporating life insurance, stock options, retirement programs, IRAs, 401(k) and profit sharing into estate plans, Marilyn's guidance helps clients protect their heirs and closely-held companies to ensure smooth succession.

Marilyn's expertise also includes special knowledge regarding estate planning as it affects those with long-term disabilities—for example, how to ensure the ability to inherit without losing other benefits. Involved in this specialized area for years, she co-authored an article on the subject of protecting the disabled person's access to public benefits with special needs trusts.

In addition, Marilyn handles an array of business planning and transaction projects for both small and large businesses. Her experience includes determining the proper entity and setting up the business, as well as tax planning and legal structure. Marilyn's work also extends to contracts, mergers and acquisitions, and the purchase and sale of assets.

# CONTENTS

# PREFACE

## *The End of a Life, the Beginning of a Life*

All marriages end. We live in a society where around half of first marriages end in divorce, but even the longest and happiest marriages end someday when "death us do part." The death of a spouse causes a sudden transition from being a married person to becoming a single person again, perhaps after many years of marriage.

According to the United States Census, the average age of widowhood for women in this country is 56. This fact indicates that many people are widowed relatively early in life as well as in later decades. This book is written for widowed men and women of all ages and in varying financial and life circumstances. The purpose of this book is to provide a guide for newly widowed women and men and their friends and family members on legal and practical issues that arise as a result of the death of a spouse.

This book will provide a guide through the first two years after a spouse's death, when many important decisions need to be made that will impact the rest of the surviving spouse's life and the lives of the couple's children. There are a few decisions that must be made immediately, and those will be pointed out, but many can and should wait for a while. Many of the chapters give practical suggestions for how friends and family can help a newly widowed person cope with grief, loss, and the need to rebuild a life as a single person.

This book may be of interest to people whose spouses are ill and who can foresee that they will be widowed in the fairly near future. If there is a little time to plan before an expected death, please read Chapter 15 on Estate Planning to be sure that all necessary estate planning has been done to avoid as many legal problems as possible.

Because this book is written for a broad audience, it is unlikely that all of the chapters will apply to all readers. The following is a summary of what is included in the various chapters so readers can choose the chapters that apply to them.

# Acknowledgements

I would like to acknowledge the constant support of my husband Ed McWilliams and our three children, Kate MacDonald, Sarah McWilliams, and Anne McWilliams, who have enriched our lives beyond measure.

In addition, I have had the great good fortune to have been influenced by a number of wise, ethical, and inspirational attorneys who have been my mentors and role models in the practice of law. I want to particularly recognize three of them, beginning with my father-in-law, Judge Robert H. McWilliams, who has devoted his life to the causes of justice and legal and human rights and has served as a worthy example for generations of attorneys and judges in Colorado. The second is the late Richard B. Elrod, who took me under his wing as a new attorney and taught me so much about how to practice law and how to do so while maintaining the highest ethical and professional standards with compassion and humanity. The third is John E. Moye, who has been a teacher and mentor for law students and practicing attorneys in Colorado for three decades and who continues to serve as an example of an attorney of the highest ethical standards and professional ability and with whom I am fortunate to practice law.

I also want to thank my clients for the opportunity to be a part of their lives. They have taught me so much about courage, wisdom, and the wide scope of the human condition.

# CHAPTER 1
# PLANNING THE FUNERAL

## § 1.1 Funerals

This discussion is aimed toward widowed people and their families and friends who find themselves needing to plan a funeral. If you are very fortunate, you and your spouse discussed this issue earlier in your lives and even may have pre-planned your funeral and burial or cremation. Our culture does not encourage speaking of death, though, and many couples never get around to a conversation on the issue. If your spouse was ill for a period of time prior to death, then you may have had the opportunity to talk about funeral planning; but many seriously ill people are too upset by this topic and feel that by discussing it they are giving up hope.

Planning a funeral is like planning any other large ceremonial or religious gathering, except that the person planning it is often very upset and unable to think clearly. Widowed people often feel that they cannot bear to attend a funeral or memorial service or want to delay it for several weeks or months because they simply cannot function well enough to plan one shortly after a death.

In general, I think it is emotionally helpful for family members and friends to have a funeral or memorial service to mark a death and to ceremonially say goodbye to the person who has died. I also think that the service should be held within a week or so of a death and not deferred into the future. A funeral does serve the purpose of marking an important life transition. It will not really be easier to plan the funeral if you wait for several weeks, and it actually makes the family feel that they are marking time until the funeral. If you feel that planning the funeral is beyond your capabilities, ask for help from family, friends, and clergy and let them help you to the extent you need. After a death, many people want to do something to help and will offer to do so.

Many religious congregations have auxiliaries or guilds or other volunteer committees that help plan funerals and provide refreshments at the site after the service. Families sometimes prefer to host a gathering after the service at home or at a club, university building, or other larger site. This kind of a gathering will require catering and planning on very short notice and you should certainly enlist the help of your friends and relatives who are experienced in planning social occasions. Do not feel obliged to produce an elaborate event at this time in your life if it feels too difficult or just does not seem right. Some type of gathering with some kind of refreshments is typical after a service and does provide an opportunity for friends, relatives, and co-workers of the deceased to reconnect with each other and to remember happy times with the deceased.

People instinctively recognize that a spouse's funeral will probably be long remembered and may be the last public statement about the spouse's life. You may be concerned about making the "right" choices about the process in order to adequately honor your spouse's life and to meet family members' expectations. Try not to burden yourself by agonizing over various decisions and let your friends and family help you. You should not, however, let other people dictate what you should do in this sensitive situation.

An additional source of stress is that funeral and burial costs can be much higher than many people expect. If your spouse had a funeral plan in place with a mortuary, have someone contact that mortuary. I have found that even with prepaid plans, there are usually some further expenses that must be paid. If there was no prearranged plan, someone needs to contact a funeral home to begin the arrangements. This might be you or a relative, friend, or clergy. Mortuaries, by law, must itemize their services and fees and make disclosures regarding many issues, including any requirement for embalming and caskets if the person is to be cremated. The mortuary must disclose in writing any costs it is incurring on your behalf (limousines, obituary notices, death certificates, flowers, service programs, police escorts, etc.). You should expect to be required to pay most or all of the cost of the mortuary's services in advance or to provide a credit card against which the costs can be charged. Mortuaries often accept assignments of life insurance policy proceeds as payment.

## § 1.2 Autopsy

Autopsies are not usually required after a death, but you may be asked for permission to perform an autopsy if your spouse's cause of death is not clear. You usually have the right to deny permission, but if you do not otherwise have clear knowledge about your spouse's cause of death, then you might want to give your consent so that you can know the truth. Be forewarned, however, that in some cases even an autopsy does not provide a conclusive diagnosis of the cause of death.

## § 1.3 Burial

If you choose burial rather than cremation, you will need to select a cemetery and plot. If you live in an area where there are several choices, you can compare costs and maintenance arrangements. Embalming before burial or cremation is not always required, although it may be in many cases by state law. Some religious groups oppose it. The funeral director must give you a written statement telling you whether embalming is required or is optional.

Some families and religious groups usually have a viewing of the body in an open casket either at the funeral or before it at the mortuary. If this is your preference and you have young children, be sure to discuss this issue with them well before this experience and do not compel or pressure a reluctant child to view the body of a deceased parent if he or she does not want to.

If your spouse was a veteran, you may be able to choose a burial site at a National Cemetery, including a memorial marker and flag to drape the coffin, free of charge. You will need to provide your spouse's honorable discharge, Social Security number, branch of service, rank, entry date, and discharge date. Spouses of veterans who are buried in private cemeteries can apply for a burial allowance, a flag, and partial reimbursement for a memorial marker.

## § 1.4 Cremation

Cremation is increasingly chosen instead of burial. Some religious groups have traditionally objected to cremation, so if you are unsure of how this issue is viewed in your faith community, consult with clergy. If you are planning a funeral service with the body present, you can rent a casket for this short-term use. If you choose direct cremation, you can choose an unfinished wooden box or other alternative container rather than a traditional (and more expensive) casket.

Many churches now offer columbariums, places in the church or on the grounds where ashes may be permanently deposited after cremation with a memorial plaque showing the person's name and dates of birth and death. Some families object to cremation because they will not have an actual grave to visit in the future, and a columbarium offers a place to come in the future to remember and honor the deceased. Some families also make donations to a house of worship to purchase a window or other religious article in memory of a deceased person so that there will be a visible memorial to the person's life. The Denver Botanic Gardens and the Park People provide park benches and other memorials in acknowledgement of donations in honor of a decedent.

In many cases, families scatter ashes at a place that the deceased particularly enjoyed in life, often in a mountain setting in Colorado. In any event, if you choose cremation, be aware that you will be given the ashes and will need to make a decision about what to do with them.

## § 1.5 Choosing a Mortuary/Funeral Director

Unless you have prior experience planning funerals or knowledge of factors influencing your choice, you may simply choose a mortuary in the area where you live. Your clergy may recommend one or a friend or relative may recommend for or against a particular business based on personal experience.

There are facilities in Colorado that only provide cremation and market themselves as lower-cost alternatives to traditional mortuaries. You probably do not feel much like comparison shopping for this service, but since costs may be high, you might ask a friend or relative to do some investigating for you. There is a widespread perception that funeral directors prey on the emotions of bereaved people in an effort to convince them to spend more money on their services than they otherwise would. While we hope this does not happen, you have every right to communicate to a funeral director that you are feeling pressured and to reiterate your own desires and budget. In my work preparing estate tax returns where funeral expenses are taken as tax deductions, I often see funeral expenses in the range of $8,000 to $10,000.

## § 1.6 Funeral or Memorial Service

Our society generally refers to services in connection with the burial of the dead as a funeral. There may or may not be a graveside service in connection with a funeral held in a house of worship. Memorial services are held in memory of the deceased and may be exactly like funerals, but there is not a burial connected with the service. As cremation becomes more common, memorial services are also increasingly common.

If either a funeral or memorial service is held in a house of worship, you will need to consult with clergy prior to making plans. Many clergy have strong preferences as to the conduct of services and some religious groups have doctrinal rules governing certain aspects of the funeral, burial, and cremation process. Some families want friends or relatives to give eulogies in honor of the deceased. In some faith communities this is discouraged or limited in length. Sometimes families would like a friend or relative to sing a solo or would like to hire a professional singer. Be aware that your house of worship might not permit this and ask the clergy before asking someone to sing or give a eulogy. In many Christian congregations, you will have the option of requesting a communion service or Mass in connection with the funeral or memorial service, and in some congregations will be strongly encouraged to do so.

Unfortunately, sometimes homes of the deceased are burglarized during the funeral or memorial service after a funeral notice has been published. It is probably a good idea to ask a trusted person to stay in your home during the service as a precaution.

## § 1.7 Obituaries and Funeral Notices

Newspapers in Colorado increasingly charge a fee for publishing obituaries and funeral notices. If there is to be a funeral or memorial service, be sure the funeral notice can be published in time for people to learn of the service and attend it. Funeral directors and clergy often help with this process. You should be prepared to provide the following information about your spouse:

- Full name of deceased.
- Name of current spouse and any prior predeceased spouse.
- Date of marriage to surviving spouse.
- Names and places of residence of children and grandchildren.
- Names and places of residence of surviving parents and brothers and sisters of the deceased.

- Date and place of birth.

- Education and degrees.

- Profession.

- Honors, awards, community service contributions, and political offices.

- Membership in organizations (social clubs, charitable groups, fraternities and sororities, and the like).

- Military service and honors.

- Hobbies and interests.

- A photograph, if desired.

## § 1.8 Flowers and Memorial Gifts

Some families believe that flowers are too expensive and too fleeting a tribute to the deceased. If you feel this way, you can certainly make your wishes known. Many people prefer that charitable donations be made in honor of the deceased. If your spouse had a cause he or she supported, that organization would be ideal to designate as a suggested recipient of memorial gifts. Otherwise, a school or university attended by the deceased, a religious organization, medical organization, or any charitable organization supporting causes of interest to the deceased would be appropriate. I have known people to make gifts of books to the library at the schools attended by children or grandchildren of the deceased, sometimes on subjects of particular interest to the deceased or to the children or grandchildren.

## § 1.9 Obtaining Death Certificates

The mortuary will order death certificates for you. It is less expensive to order as many as you think you might need all at one time, although you can order more from the health department later if necessary. You will need death certificates for many purposes, including making claims for life insurance, retirement plans, veterans benefits, Social Security benefits, and health insurance continuation benefits; changing title to vehicles, real estate, investment accounts, stocks, bonds, mutual funds, and bank accounts; and closing credit card accounts in the name of the deceased.

You will need to provide the following information for the death certificate:

- Full name of the deceased.
- Date of birth.
- Date of death.
- Place of birth.
- Names of mother (maiden name) and father.
- Place of death.
- Social Security number.

## § 1.10 Children and Funerals

People offer conflicting advice about whether young children should attend the funeral of a parent. Reluctant children should never be forced to attend a parent's funeral, but many children who are not permitted to attend a parent's funeral express regret in later life that they were kept away. In general, all children should be encouraged to view a funeral as a way of honoring the person who has died.

Very young children need very basic explanations about what a funeral is. They need to be told exactly what will happen, including a description of details of the ritual, whether or not the parent's body will be present at the site of the funeral, whether or not a hearse will arrive with a casket—and in fact, what a hearse is. Explain to the children what a eulogy is, that there will be a procession to or from the church and from the cemetery, and whether or not there will be a burial service and/or a reception following the funeral.

Children also need to understand that if there is a reception following the funeral, people will be telling stories and perhaps jokes about the deceased. They should be told that these people will be trying to remember happy times they had with the person, and that their intent is not to be irreverent or insulting. Children should also be told that sometimes at funerals adults become very sad and cry and that they may wear special clothing and what it will look like.

## § 1.11 Expressions of Gratitude

Widowed persons often receive cards, letters, flowers, food, and memorial gifts in honor of their deceased spouses. All of these are expressions of affection, respect, and concern for the surviving spouse. Someone should be delegated the job of keeping a notebook with a list of all of these acts of kindness, including who the sender is. A notebook should also be kept by the phone to make a list of the people who call. As soon as possible, write a short personal note to all of the people who did any of these things. Their kindness should be acknowledged as a matter or courtesy, but it also helps keep the widowed person in contact with others and aware of how many people care about them.

## § 1.12 Timeline

Following is a list of tasks that you should plan to take care of in the year following your spouse's death:

Immediately:

- Locate documents—birth certificate for yourself and minor children; marriage license; Social Security numbers for your spouse, yourself, and your children; bank records; life insurance policies; military records.

- Notify family and friends of spouse's death and funeral arrangements (consider delegating this task to a friend or relative), and keep a record of who has been contacted.

- Keep all incoming mail for later review and use.

- Get information on health insurance for yourself and minor children.

First Month:

- Get state-certified copies of the death certificate (usually ordered from the funeral home). Generally, ten copies should suffice.

- Select an attorney experienced in estate administration and tax matters.

- Apply for benefits from life insurance, Social Security, the Department of Veterans Affairs, employer pensions, and annuities.

- Before paying any major expense, do a thorough analysis of available assets and total liabilities and defer payment (if possible) until the analysis is complete; pay mortgages, health insurance premiums, and any other truly essential expenses; and make sure your home and vehicles remain insured.

- Plan a temporary budget.

Within Six Months:

- Thoroughly investigate the location and value of your assets; contact banks, spouse's employer, investment advisors and brokers, and retirement plan administrators.

- Engage an accountant and commence tax and financial planning. Provide complete financial information to both your attorney and accountant and be sure they both know you have engaged both of them.

- Work with your attorney to commence estate and trust administration, including ordering appraisals of personal items (household goods, vehicles, art, jewelry, etc.) and of real estate and private business.

- Analyze where you are living to determine if the cost makes it urgent for you to move; delay this decision for at least a year, if possible.

- Work with your accountant and other financial advisors to determine the status of assets, liabilities, and needs; defer major decisions if possible.n Consider joining a support group and/or obtain private grief counseling and support for yourself and your children.

- Review the status of periodic expenses such as property tax, vehicle and homeowner's insurance, and vehicle leases.

- Work with your attorney and accountant to determine whether or not a federal estate tax return (and one or more state estate or inheritance tax returns) need to be prepared and if tax will be due—and if so, the source of funds for payment.

- Work with your attorney and accountant to determine the status of your spouse's income tax returns and payments and work with them to prepare any upcoming income tax returns.

- Work with your attorney to decide if any assets should be disclaimed, and if so, be sure the proper documentation is prepared.

At Nine Months:

- Be sure any required federal and state estate and inheritance tax returns are filed and tax payment is made.

- Be sure any disclaimers are filed.

At One Year:

- Be sure your own estate planning is current and adequate; obtain life insurance if necessary for the support of children or for other necessary purposes.

# CHAPTER 2
# EARLY DAYS

## § 2.1 Accepting Help From Family and Friends

At the death of a spouse, whether sudden or expected due to illness, many surviving spouses feel unable to function or, on the contrary, feel fully competent but really are not. This is one time in life to accept offers of help from other people and not feel guilty about needing it. People often do not know what to do to help a widowed person, and the widow(er) does not feel comfortable making suggestions.

It might be a good idea to contact one or two people who are very close to you (and who are well-organized and calm) and ask them to help coordinate arrangements with you. The first—and emotionally difficult—task is to let other people know of the death. You do not have to take on this burden except to call immediate family members. Give your helpers your spouse's personal phone list, your holiday card list, and any other lists of people who should be notified, and ask them to call as soon as possible. While this is difficult news to deliver, people involved with your spouse's life need and want to know as soon as possible.

I have seen people provide the following acts of support to widowed people, which were much appreciated:

- Contacting the employer of a decedent who was still working at the time of death and beginning to collect benefit information.
- Accompanying the widowed spouse to make funeral and burial or cremation plans.
- Planning a reception after the service.
- Preparing and delivering meals to the home (this is particularly convenient if they can be frozen for later use).
- Coordinating a calendar so that friends bring in dinner every night for several weeks.

- Planning to pick up out-of-town relatives at the airport and making hotel reservations for them.

- Providing transportation for young children to school and after-school activities.

- Providing pet care.

- Coordinating house cleaning and lawn care.

- Taking turns staying at the house (and answering the phone and door) so the newly widowed person will not be alone.

- Helping collect financial information.

- Helping locate an appropriate attorney.

- Helping clean out the office of a decedent who was still working at time of death.

Your friends genuinely want to help you at this time in your life, and most people are happy to do anything you ask of them. It might be easier for someone else to suggest the things you need, including the tasks listed above, so feel free to let your helpers suggest ways people can help if they ask.

## § 2.2 Helping Your Children

If you have young children, they need your support—even if you feel that you cannot make the situation all right. No one will be able to make the situation all right, so the best you can do is to be with your children, be aware of their needs, and let them know how much you love them. A more detailed discussion of this topic is provided in Chapter 12. The children's school principal and friends' parents should be notified of the death. If your children want to participate in funeral planning, let them do so and keep them informed as to what is going on. You should address your young children's needs as your highest priority. In some cases, the widowed surviving parent is in such distress that the children are ignored, with devastating emotional effects at the time and later in life. Get whatever help and support you need from others to help you help your children.

If your children are adults, you all need to support each other. You should feel no reluctance to ask them for what you need. Recognize, however, that they may be so upset themselves that someone else would be a better choice to assist you.

## § 2.3 Beginning to Organize Financial and Legal Matters

Unfortunately, practical concerns arise at a time when you feel least capable of coping with such issues. Many widowed people feel a sense of panic about financial issues on the death of a spouse. Many women are interested in financial matters, have a career in business, and are fully informed on the family finances, but it is still quite common that men in a marriage manage the money and property. On the contrary, in some marriages, the woman handles all the finances. In many marriages, one spouse or the other simply finds financial matters boring or confusing and prefers to let the other spouse handle those areas for the family rather than learning about or dealing with those issues. Regardless of gender, if you are not the person who was accustomed to handling the finances, then you may feel anxious about every aspect of your future.

A fundamental misconception is that a lot of important decisions need to be made very quickly. In fact, most financial matters can (and should) be deferred until a calmer time, at least a few months into the future. I am not suggesting that these matters be ignored, but that only the truly essential issues be dealt with in the immediate aftermath of a death. I have seen many newly widowed people make financial decisions soon after the death of a spouse, which they later greatly regretted. I have been told by widowed people that they do not even remember making decisions or the reasons they made them in the first months after the death of a spouse. Some widowed persons need a lot of education about financial matters in order to make prudent decisions and are in no condition to take on learning about topics that do not greatly interest them at a time when they are terribly upset emotionally.

Try to remain calm and do not let anyone rush you into decisions that can wait, such as how to invest or spend life insurance. In many cases, you will need to collect a lot of information and then find appropriate advice and take the time you need to decide what to do. Some decisions can be deferred for a year or more. Many people offer well-intended financial advice and recommend financial planners. Some relatives, friends, and financial advisors make widowed people feel that they must take action immediately. This is almost never true, and is sometimes an attempt to take advantage of a bereaved person. Sometimes adult children or other friends and relatives offer to take over all the financial matters for a widowed person. In some cases this can be helpful and appropriate, but in others it can result in an unnecessary loss of autonomy. For the short term, help with organizing and collecting financial information is probably appropriate, but a decision to permanently turn over control of a person's finances can wait for a thorough analysis in a few months.

There are some practical actions you can take, though, to be sure that important information and decisions do not get lost. If your spouse had more than one mailing address, use a post office form to change the mailing address so that all the mail comes to your home. In order not to lose or miss important information that comes in the mail, get a number of large manila envelopes and label them with different categories. Put the mail each day into the appropriate envelope and keep it until you are able to review it or have someone else review it for you. If you have someone close to you who you trust to handle financial matters, that person could review the mail for you and let you know if anything is truly urgent, but I would recommend that the actual mail remain at your home rather than being taken elsewhere.

## § 2.3.1 What Is Necessary

There are some things that need to be attended to fairly quickly. It is vitally important that all forms of insurance on your life, health, home, and vehicles be maintained, which means paying premiums as they become due. Be sure that your spouse's employer forwards his or her mail to you promptly, since some insurance notices may come to the workplace.

If your spouse was receiving Social Security, the Social Security Administration must be notified of the death right away. They will require a full refund for any payment made for the month of death, no matter how many days the deceased lived during that month. Many mortuaries contact Social Security on behalf of the family of the deceased, but it is your responsibility to make sure that this is done. It is against the law to continue to collect Social Security on behalf of someone who is no longer living.

If you are covered by health insurance through your spouse's employer, inquire or ask someone else to inquire about your rights to continue coverage.

If you are covered by an individual policy or a Medicare supplemental policy, be sure the premiums are paid. This is a crucial issue for your welfare.

If you are renting a home, continue to pay the rent. A sympathetic landlord may give you a grace period, but do not expect it to last very long. If you have a mortgage, make the monthly payments if you can. Do not make an immediate decision to pay off the balance of the mortgage; this decision can wait until you get a complete financial picture and can thoughtfully create a budget. If you cannot make the payment, contact the lender and explain the situation. If you receive a notice that the lender is foreclosing on the house, contact the lender immediately. If you do not know if there is a mortgage on your home, it is essential to find out. A bill may come in the mail, but it is common to have a coupon book that the borrower uses to pay each month. Many people have mortgage payments made automatically from their bank accounts. Your attorney can order a search of the county real estate records to determine whether or not your home secures a loan. This is an important issue, and people are sometimes surprised to learn that a spouse mortgaged the home without the other spouse's knowledge.

If you do not have immediate access to money to live on, it will be necessary for you to accelerate the information-gathering process to determine the assets available from your deceased spouse. If you have your own funds, you can take longer to collect complete financial information.

If you do not already know, you should try to find out if your spouse had a will. People often keep wills in bank safe deposit boxes, so contact the bank your spouse used to find out if he or she had a safe deposit box. People also often leave wills in their attorney's custody, so if your spouse had an attorney, call the attorney and ask for this information.

To be valid, wills must be originally signed documents and must comply with other legal requirements. People sometimes find a photocopy of a will or an unsigned draft of a will or a will form on a computer. These are not valid wills, but may indicate that a will was prepared and may give clues as to where the original is located. A majority of people in this country, however, die without a will. If you find a will, be aware that under Colorado law, wills must be "lodged" with the court in the county where the deceased person lived within ten days of death. You can do this yourself, or contact an estate administration attorney to help you through the process. You will need to make copies of the will. Court personnel can give you some help, but they are not permitted to give legal advice.

You will probably need to find out rather quickly if you have access to your spouse's bank accounts as a joint owner. If not, and if you do not have sufficient funds of your own, you will need to get legal assistance soon.

Some people have life insurance through an employer, as a veteran or through a private policy. Your spouse's employer's human resources department will be able to give information about these policies. You can get veterans insurance information by contacting the Department of Veterans Affairs (www.va.gov). It sometimes takes longer to discover whether or not a spouse had private life insurance. You might find policy information in your spouse's financial records, or premiums may be paid automatically from bank accounts (look for the information on bank statements). Policies are often kept in safe deposit boxes, home file cabinets, and desks, and many estate planning attorneys have records of their clients' life insurance policies. You will need claim forms and death certificates to make insurance claims. Insurance companies have claims departments you can reach by phone, and most have websites that can help direct you to the correct contact to make a claim.

If your spouse owned a business or a partial interest in a business, you should at least address the short-term continuing operation of the business without your spouse's services. This is one of the most difficult issues for a surviving spouse who was not involved in running the business during the deceased spouse's lifetime. There is a more detailed discussion of this issue in Chapter 6. Be aware, however, that in some cases, taking immediate action can save the business and on the contrary, not taking prompt action can cause a business to simply close and lose the value it otherwise could have provided the family. If this issue applies to you, contact the business attorney used by the business, if any. If there are other business owners, contact your own attorney to represent your interests as soon as possible.

If your spouse was killed in an accident of any kind, it will be in your best interest to contact an attorney right away to protect your rights. This is true whether the accident was caused by your spouse or by someone else. You should also contact any applicable insurance carrier, such as automobile or homeowner's insurance. Many people are not aware that homeowner's insurance will provide legal defense in many kinds of situations, but only if they are notified promptly of a problem. In most cases, you cannot be sued for an accident you did not cause; but your deceased spouse's estate can be sued for an accident your spouse caused, and this can have an enormous impact on your future. Do not sign a release or settlement agreement without consulting an attorney who is well versed in cases involving accidental death.

## § 2.3.2 What Can or Should Be Deferred

You will probably make better decisions about many issues later rather than sooner. Many widowed people immediately think about moving or are encouraged to do so by adult children or others. If at all possible, defer this decision for a year or longer. The death of a spouse is one of the most difficult and stressful events that ever happens in life. Why add the stress of a move to an already difficult situation?

I believe that some people think life will be less painful if they are not surrounded by everyday reminders of the deceased spouse. Anyone who has ever tried to escape emotional pain by changing the scenery can tell you that this will not work. It will simply remove you from your comfortable, familiar surroundings and your social support system. Your memories of your spouse and your grief over the death will be with you wherever you are. If, however, you realize that you must move because there is no possibility that you can afford to continue to live where you are without your spouse's income, then give yourself permission to ask for and accept as much help as possible during this difficult process.

Many widowed people are contacted soon after their spouse's death by financial advisors and urged to make decisions about what to do with life insurance proceeds and retirement plan accounts. Life insurance can be paid to you in a lump sum or through other options offered by the company. You do not have to make a decision about what to do with the money in any particular time period. Unless you are an experienced and sophisticated investor, you will need to gather information and educate yourself before making decisions. Some investments will never be appropriate for you and some tie up money for a long time, which might not be in your best interest. I have seen investment advisors suggest wildly risky and inappropriate investments to newly widowed people who are financially unsophisticated, so proceed with caution.

There are special and very technical rules about the timing of distributions from retirement plans and individual retirement accounts (IRAs), which are discussed in Chapter 7. The complexity of these rules can cause people to make some expensive mistakes in dealing with these assets, so get advice from an attorney or an accountant who is well versed in this area and do not make snap decisions about what to do with these assets. Be aware, though, that some decisions do need to be made in limited time periods, and get some professional advice on this issue within six months or so following the death.

# CHAPTER 3
# GETTING EMOTIONAL SUPPORT

## § 3.1 Grief

Grief caused by the death of a spouse is a normal, natural, and painful reaction to a loss not only of an individual's life, but also of the relationship and the life the two of you created together. Grief is hard because it brings intense emotions, including sadness, fear, relief, anger, or compassion. Some widowed people say they feel like they are drowning in pain.

## § 3.2 Phases of Grief

The initial phase of grief is disbelief and shock immediately following the death. Even if a spouse was known to be terminally ill, the actual fact of death is a shock—and the shock can be much worse if the death was unexpected. There is often a perception of unreality; that this cannot really be happening.

In the next phase, an awareness of just how great the loss really is and intense feelings of grief arise. There is difficulty sleeping and uncontrollable weeping.

There can follow a period of feeling panicked, mental instability, and physical symptoms such as headache, upset stomach, lightheadedness, throat constriction, inability to concentrate, aimless restlessness, sleep disturbance, and lack of appetite.

Feelings of guilt arise over a perceived failure to have done enough for the deceased spouse or a failure to prevent what happened. Many widowed people feel great anger over what they believe caused the death of their spouse.

People feel unable to function, concentrate, or resume normal activities. Grief has taken over their life and there is no "normal" part of life for a while.

After a time—which can be a very long time—a reconciliation of the grief comes gradually and a sense of peace and normalcy returns in fits and starts. This phase is like healing from a physical wound and takes some people longer than others. Our culture is uncomfortable with grieving that takes "too long."

But eventually, a sense of hope returns and life once again has meaning and even joy.

## § 3.3 Caring for Yourself

You need to make taking care of yourself your primary task in the early days and do what helps you, even if other people do not understand. People are uncomfortable with grief and may try to rush you to return to "normal" and stop talking about your spouse. Americans expect people to be strong and stoic, but recovery from grief takes longer than many people expect. The grieving process is individual, and no one has the right to tell you that you are taking too long to recover.

Feel free to cry as much as you want. Talk about your spouse and seek out people who are willing to listen to you for as long as you need to talk about what happened and your stories about him or her and your life together. Read your love letters and look at pictures of your spouse.

Take care of your health. Try to eat a healthy diet. Go for walks or swim. Resist overindulging in alcohol. Accept that there will be some bad days and some better days, and that this will go on for a long time.

As I state many times in this book, postpone making important decisions. Almost everything can wait, no matter what some people tell you.

## § 3.4 Sources of Support

### § 3.4.1 Family and Friends

This is not the time to prove how strong you are. Accept help from any source. You can pay it back later by offering support and help to other people in need.

If you have family, gather them together and support each other. Even if there have been differences in the past, this is the time to forgive and to join together to help each other.

Friends genuinely want to help, but often are afraid to intrude on a newly widowed person. Sometimes people make inappropriate statements such as "I know just how you feel" or begin reciting their own stories of bereavement. The most helpful attitude is to have faith that people mean well and to take them up on their offers of help. Sometimes one very close family member or friend takes on the role of spokesperson for the family and can "run interference" for the newly widowed person who is too upset or overwhelmed to communicate with a lot of people.

As mentioned in Chapter 2, an essential task that must be taken up immediately is notifying other people of a death. No one wants to hear this news, but it is worse not to know something has happened to a close family member, friend, or co-worker than it is to receive the information and be able to act appropriately. Some people are very hurt to read of a death in the newspaper before being contacted by the family if they considered the deceased to be a close friend.

Assign one person or a small number of people to call people who were important in your spouse's life. Names can be obtained from personal phone lists, holiday card lists, business Rolodexes, or computer files. Family members must be told first. Employers and co-workers should also be told right away.

If friends offer to help, the family spokesperson should be ready with a list of tasks that would be helpful. These could include picking up people coming for the funeral from the airport and helping to arrange for their lodging, car rental, or other transportation needs. People often offer to bring food to the family. It can be helpful for one person to coordinate food gifts to arrange for a meal or snacks after the funeral. Some families prefer to have a caterer provide the food and drink for a gathering after the funeral, and many churches have volunteer groups that provide the food as part of the church's ministry to the bereaved, so no one should assume these arrangements without checking with the widow first.

It is also considerate for a friend to set up a calendar for friends and family to sign up for a specific date to bring meals to the family for a period of time after the funeral. Gifts of main dishes and soups that can be frozen and then brought out for an easy meal sometime in the next few weeks are most welcome.

Some kind and caring groups of friends have turned themselves into "cleaning crews" who come to the home together to clean and tidy the house in a short period of time so the family doesn't have to be concerned with this mundane task. Friends can take charge of lawn care, snow removal, and even pet care. If the family has children, friends can offer to take over the car-pooling duties for school, sports, and other activities for a while.

An offer to take a walk with the newly widowed person can be comforting if he or she feels up to it. A walk offers a little moderate exercise along with conversation. People will inquire as to charities to which they can make memorial gifts, so a list should be kept by the telephone. A notebook should be kept by the phone as well, and whoever answers the phone should make a note of the date and time of each call with the name of the caller.

Someone should be in charge of collecting and keeping all sympathy cards and letters (with the envelopes attached to reference the address of each sender) for reading and re-reading in the future. Newly widowed people are often in such a state of emotional shock that they cannot focus very clearly on these messages soon after a death, but find that they are comforting to read again in the weeks and months that follow. Many widows find it comforting to send thank-you notes to all the people who sent flowers, memorial gifts, food, cards, and letters as a way to connect again with the people who were important to their spouse.

## § 3.4.2 Support Groups, Individual Counseling, and Medication

Many faith communities offer grief support groups for adults and children. Clergy are often trained to provide individual counseling as well. Community organizations and hospitals sometimes offer grief support groups and other resources. Some of the organizations are identified in the Appendix to this book.

For many people, while support groups are helpful, they are not enough to allow them to return to a fairly normal routine of life. If this is your case, consult with your doctor and discuss the option of individual counseling with a trained professional and the pros and cons of taking antidepressant medication, at least for a trial period. You do not have to go through this experience alone.

Your grieving process is individual to you and you must not let pride or other people prevent you from doing whatever you need to do to take care of yourself. There is no right or wrong way to grieve this loss. Bereavement is a process by which you learn to live without a spouse, but hold on to the memories of the life you had together.

# CHAPTER 4
# LEGAL ASSISTANCE

## § 4.1 Do You Need an Attorney?

In the majority of cases, the surviving spouse becomes responsible for the administration of the deceased spouse's estate. This is because (1) people typically name their spouse as Personal Representative (sometimes referred to as "executor" or "executrix") in wills; and (2) in the case of an intestate estate (*i.e.*, where the person died without a will), state law gives priority for the surviving spouse to be appointed as the Personal Representative. This chapter is written assuming that you as a surviving spouse will be serving as Personal Representative of your deceased spouse's estate. Even if you are not acting in that capacity, you may want to hire an attorney to represent your interests as an heir or beneficiary.

Be aware that the attorney who does the probate and estate administration is legally presumed to represent the Personal Representative, not the individual beneficiaries, unless a different arrangement is made in writing. The estate attorney has the obligation of advising the Personal Representative on how to administer the estate in the best interests of all the beneficiaries, not just the surviving spouse.

### § 4.1.1 Why You May Need an Attorney

As a newly widowed person, you may have extremely serious needs for an attorney in certain circumstances, such as if your spouse was killed in an accident. In most other cases, however, you will benefit from at least a consultation with an experienced estate administration and probate attorney. In general, the fewer assets involved in an estate and the fewer family members, the simpler the administration of the estate.

There are important issues that good attorneys can spot—and which few lay people are aware of—that can make a big difference in your life in the future. You don't know what you don't know. A good attorney with an adequate background in estate administration law can save you and your family large amounts of money. This is true even if your spouse did no estate planning, although a better result is almost always achieved by appropriate estate planning.

Another reason you should at least consult an attorney is that you are likely not in an emotional condition at this time in your life to take on a project that will require a lot of detail work and learning new facts. A well-staffed law firm will be able to take care of locating and collecting assets for you far faster than you would by yourself in most cases. Attorneys and paralegals who regularly practice estate administration law are able to review bank records and tax returns to discover assets you might not be aware of. They also will have contact information for insurance companies and investment brokers and will be able to expedite claims for these assets. If you are going to be selling real estate through a probate estate, then someone will need to open probate and have an attorney prepare a Personal Representative deed for the transfer. Title insurance companies will not prepare Personal Representative deeds.

Someone will need to determine whether or not a federal (and one or more state) estate tax returns are necessary for your spouse's estate. If you are the Personal Representative of the estate, you are personally liable to the IRS for preparing these tax returns, which are quite different from the income tax returns most people are familiar with. Qualified estate administration attorneys can advise you on this issue, provided that they have knowledge of taxation.

One unfortunate result of all of the blended families in this country is that there are many grounds for conflict between a second or subsequent surviving spouse and the children of the decedent's earlier marriage, whether the children are minors or adults. Minor children may have legal rights to support from the estate of a deceased parent, whether or not the parent provided for this in an estate plan. If this is your situation, litigation is possible over this issue. If your deceased spouse left adult children from another marriage, litigation can result from a lack of estate planning or if either you or the children are unhappy over the estate plan of the deceased spouse.

Sometimes people forget to change the beneficiary designations for life insurance, retirement plans, or IRAs after a new marriage, and leave a former spouse or children from an earlier marriage as beneficiaries of these assets rather than a current spouse. These assets can be quite valuable, and an attorney can help you analyze whether you can take any action to claim them;

often you can. Second and subsequent marriages are quite common among widowed people, and this trend is increasing since people are living longer than they once did.

In analyzing whether or not you need an attorney to help administer your spouse's estate, it is simply logical that people who spend every day of their working lives administering estates are likely to be more knowledgeable than people who do not. Depending on your situation, you may need very little help from an attorney or a great deal of help, but you are likely to benefit from at least a consultation.

If your spouse was involved in any kind of litigation prior to death, had significant debts, died in an accident, owned a business or a partial interest in a business, owned real estate in another state, or was having any controversy with the IRS or any other taxing authority, you definitely need legal assistance.

### § 4.1.2 Why You Might Not Need an Attorney

While I believe that almost every widowed person should at least consult with an attorney, there are some cases where there is not much need for legal help. For example, you probably do not need an attorney if your spouse had very few assets with very little financial value and they were owned in joint tenancy with you or you were the named beneficiary; if your spouse had little or no debt; or if your spouse did not leave minor children or adult children from another marriage. You still might want to consult an attorney to be sure you are not overlooking something that would be of benefit to you.

## § 4.2 How to Choose an Attorney

Attorneys, like doctors, are not all alike and are not interchangeable. Some are more experienced, knowledgeable, and skilled than others. Unlike doctors, who are formally trained and licensed in certain medical specialties, attorneys in Colorado and most other states are only licensed to practice law in general by the state. In Colorado, the Colorado Supreme Court licenses attorneys and has continuing oversight over them. There is no requirement, however, that allows or forbids any attorney from holding himself or herself out as having expertise in a particular area of law. Nor is there any specific course or training that is required to practice in a particular area.

There is no sanctioned way for an attorney to become a "specialist" in certain areas of the law the way doctors become specialists in specific areas of medicine. Many attorneys now focus their work on a limited number of areas and develop broad and deep knowledge in those few areas. There are, however, still attorneys who are generalists. Attorneys with specialized skills and significant experience in specific areas of the law are more common in larger communities.

All of this leaves the consumer of legal services somewhat in the dark as to how to choose an attorney. Many widowed people have never had to work with an attorney or select one before in their lives and are now faced with making an important decision at a time when they may not be thinking clearly. A competent estate administration attorney must have knowledge of both state probate and property law and have an expertise in estate tax law. Many attorneys work in both the areas of estate planning and estate administration, while others spend most of their time on one area or the other. While these areas are closely related, they are not interchangeable.

For estate administration, you will want to be sure that the attorney you use spends a significant amount of time working on estate administration matters rather than on estate *planning* matters. Some attorneys have earned both a law degree and a master's degree in taxation, called an L.L.M., which is an indication that the attorneys have knowledge about tax matters. Be warned, though, that some attorneys simply open an office with no one to train them and no coursework in estate or tax matters; they merely "learn by doing" and hold themselves out as practicing estate and trust law.

If you are the person who is solely responsible for the administration of the estate and you are the sole heir or beneficiary, then you are only responsible for what happens to you; therefore, you have great discretion in choosing an attorney. If, however, you are responsible for estate administration and you are not the sole beneficiary, then you have a serious responsibility to other people to protect their legal rights and financial welfare. This responsibility is referred to as a "fiduciary duty" in legal terms. In this case, it is prudent for you to interview at least two (and preferably three) attorneys located from different sources and gather written information from all of them as to their qualifications before selecting an attorney.

## § 4.2.1 Referrals: How They Can Help and Why They Might Not

So how do you choose an appropriate attorney? If your spouse had an estate planning attorney, that would be a logical place to start. However, this attorney may not be the person best suited to your needs in estate administration. Other people hear about an attorney from friends or relatives. This may or may not be a good referral source. If the referral is made by someone who used the attorney for estate administration work and was pleased with the experience, the referral may be appropriate. Unfortunately, sometimes lay people do not know that they are not being given good advice from an attorney and recommend someone just because they found the attorney to be pleasant. People often recommend attorneys who they have used in some other area of law. Some attorneys are under such pressure to generate fees that they take on projects they are not really qualified to do.

Whenever you interview attorneys, be sure to ask what percentage of their time they spend doing work in the area of law you need help in. You should also ask the attorney how long he or she has been practicing in that area of law. You do not necessarily need an attorney with many, many years of experience; but if the attorney has very little experience, you will want to make sure that there is a more experienced supervising attorney working on your matters as well.

If you have worked with attorneys in the past on other kinds of cases and had a good experience with them, you can ask them if their firm has an estate administration department or if they can recommend a good estate administration attorney to you. Other good sources of referrals are other professionals who come into frequent contact with attorneys, such as accountants, bankers, investment advisors, life insurance brokers, and real estate brokers.

## § 4.2.2 Legal Resource Directories

The Colorado Bar Association (CBA) publishes a statewide legal directory each year listing licensed attorneys in various areas of law. (You can call the CBA at 303-860-1115.) Attorneys do not have to be listed in the directory, but many choose to do so. The directory includes a list (with contact information) of attorneys who practice estate planning and estate administration and probate law. The CBA also maintains a website with lists of attorneys who practice in various areas (www.cobar.org).

Be aware that the CBA does not screen the attorneys on its lists. Attorneys choose where they want to be listed, so the CBA is not making endorsements of certain attorneys by placing their names on its lists. It is simply making information available to the public about attorneys who are available in certain areas of the law. Each county in Colorado also has its own local bar association, which maintains information on attorneys practicing in the county.

The Metropolitan Lawyer Referral Service offers the services of member attorneys to the public in the greater Denver metropolitan front-range area (303-831-8000 or www.mlrsonline.org). This organization requires that attorneys join and comply with certain rules prior to being listed with its program.

Martindale-Hubbell is a series of directories of attorneys published annually for each state. The directories are available at the Martindale-Hubbell website (www.martindale.com) as well as in traditional book form at various libraries, including the law libraries at the University of Colorado and the University of Denver. The Martindale-Hubbell website is quite easy to use and permits searches by geographical area, area of law, and size of law firm. Listing in Martindale-Hubbell is voluntary for attorneys and requires payment of a fee.

Less than half of the attorneys licensed in the United States are listed in Martindale-Hubbell. However, it provides more information than many directories, in that it lists the areas of law particular attorneys focus on (if the attorney wishes to state them) and it conducts peer evaluations of attorneys by mail. There is a rating system based on the peer evaluations explained in the front of the books, which rates attorneys from A to C for technical ability and has a V rating for ethics. Not every attorney listed in Martindale-Hubbell has a rating, and frequently only attorneys with the highest peer evaluation rating permit Martindale-Hubbell to publish their ratings. Some attorneys do not have ratings because they have not been in practice long enough to have established many contacts in the legal community.

Martindale-Hubbell permits attorneys to choose their own classifications as to areas of practice, so a listing in a certain category does not guarantee any particular level of skill in that area. A lack of a listing in Martindale-Hubbell or a lack of a rating should not be construed as evidence of a lack of skill or qualification of an attorney. Highly rated attorneys do tend to publish their information, including their ratings, in Martindale-Hubbell. Some consumers gain comfort from knowing that a particular attorney states in Martindale-Hubbell that he or she practices in a certain area and that the attorney has received a high peer-review evaluation.

### § 4.2.3 Advertising

Legal directories are one specialized form of advertising. Attorneys also advertise their services through listings in the yellow pages and other directories, by paying to be listed and choosing the categories under which their names appear. There is no requirement that any attorney present any evidence of any competence in a particular area of law to be listed in that category. Some very well-qualified attorneys do not advertise in the yellow pages for various reasons.

In most directories, there are categories for wills and trusts, estate planning, probate, and tax. There may also be a listing for "elder law." Many consumers assume that "elder law" encompasses all possible legal needs for elderly people. Most attorneys who list themselves as elder law practitioners have expertise in guardianships, conservatorships, estate planning, estate administration, Social Security, Medicare and Medicaid, and perhaps tax. However, some elder law attorneys focus on one or two of these areas more than others. If you need an attorney to administer an estate, one who focuses on guardianships and conservatorships probably is not the best choice for you.

Some attorneys advertise on television and radio and others advertise by mail. Advertising by attorneys is like any other kind of advertising, in that it costs money and presents a product or service to a wide audience in a positive light.

## § 4.3 Cost of Legal Services

If you have used attorneys for other purposes recently, you may be familiar with the cost of legal services. If not, and this is your first experience with an attorney, you may be apprehensive about the cost. Most attorneys bill on an hourly rate for estate administration services. Often, estate administration attorneys employ paralegals who perform many of the functions necessary to administer estates under the supervision of an attorney, but whose hourly rates are much lower than that of the attorney. Many law firms also have senior partners supervising younger attorneys who do much of the work at a lower hourly rate.

It is true that very skilled and experienced attorneys often charge more (sometimes significantly more) than $200 per hour. It is also true that some attorneys with high hourly rates are very efficient and that the total cost of their services will be no higher than that of a lower priced but less efficient attorney. If your situation is complex and requires skill, knowledge, and experience in order to solve difficult or sophisticated problems, an expert attorney can often save you significant money despite high hourly fees. For example, some estates have complex tax problems. Highly skilled tax attorneys are generally not cheap, but getting ineffective counsel can be very expensive too.

Attorney fees for an estate are a financial obligation of the estate. They are tax deductible either on a federal estate tax return or the estate's income tax return. You should expect to be asked to sign an engagement agreement setting out the terms for hiring an attorney, including how much you will be charged by the attorneys working on the administration of the estate and whether or not a paralegal will perform some of the tasks. You should expect to receive an itemized bill each month for the legal fees and other costs and expenses, such as court filing fees, copy costs, long distance phone calls, and other incidental items. The bill should contain descriptions of what services were provided. You will be expected to pay the bill in full each month, although in estate administration cases, many attorneys will agree to wait for payment until assets can be liquidated, *e.g.*, until a house or other real estate is sold, which can take some time.

## § 4.4 Interviewing an Attorney

When making an appointment to interview an attorney, you should state in advance that you are considering an engagement to administer your spouse's estate. You should expect to pay for the initial consultation, although some attorneys do not charge for an initial meeting. You should ask for written information about the attorney's qualifications. Take a copy of your spouse's will with you and as much financial and asset information as you can. This helps the attorney gauge the complexity of the estate. Be honest about any possible family conflicts you foresee, and about any creditors of your deceased spouse, including any tax problems. Estates with foreseeable legal problems or assets such as real estate or private businesses are often best served by law firms that have litigation and real estate departments in addition to estate and trust departments.

As with other professionals in life, you are likely to find some attorneys to be more personable or compatible with you than others. You should be able to locate an attorney who is both competent and pleasant to work with. If you do not find such a person after your first efforts, you may wish to look further and interview one or more other attorneys from different referral sources.

## § 4.5 What Services Can an Attorney and Legal Staff Provide?

Many law firms that offer estate and trust administration services can handle all aspects of these matters for you. Other firms prefer to delegate certain areas to other professionals, such as accountants, or to other law firms that provide services they do not. A full-service law firm should be able to offer you assistance with:

- Interpreting the will and any trusts.
- Providing legal guidance for determining the heirs of an intestate decedent and who has priority for appointment as Personal Representative.
- Locating assets in financial institutions.
- Making claims for life insurance, employee benefits, and IRAs, including tax analysis.
- Determining whether or not a probate proceeding is necessary.
- Preparing probate documents.
- Analyzing creditor claims.
- Setting up an estate (and trust, if necessary) accounting system.
- Advising you on how to comply with standards of fiduciary duty.
- Preparing estate and inheritance tax returns and estate income tax returns.
- Preparing the decedent's final income tax return or assisting an accountant with this process.

- Helping you locate other professionals if you need them (*e.g.*, appraisers, accountants, business brokers, and real estate brokers).

- Setting up guardianships and conservatorships for minor children.

- Dealing with real estate transactions.

- Defending against claims against the estate.

- Helping you prepare a plan of distribution of the estate that is equitable to all beneficiaries, and supervising this process.

- Advising on business issues for estates where there are private businesses.

## § 4.6 Legal Matters with Minor Children

Children in Colorado (and most other states) are considered adults for most purposes on their eighteenth birthday. Until that time, the law requires that they have legal representatives to take care of them and their property.

If you and your spouse had minor children, you will most certainly become their legal guardian (*i.e.*, the person who has custody of the children). If children are named as beneficiaries in a will or of an insurance policy or retirement plan or IRA, then the court will need to appoint a conservator (a person who has control of their finances) to take care of their assets until they turn 18.

Parents typically name guardians and conservators for minor children in wills. If there is no will, the surviving parent has priority for appointment. Parents sometimes set up trusts for minor children under their wills or otherwise, and name trustees to handle the children's money until they reach a certain age, which may be later than 18. The trustee may be someone other than a surviving spouse and could be a bank. Banks and trust companies can serve as conservator or trustee.

I frequently see cases where a parent or grandparent has named a minor as beneficiary of life insurance. Insurance companies will not pay life insurance proceeds to a minor. It will therefore be necessary to petition the court to appoint a conservator (or in some cases, a custodian under the Uniform Transfers to Minors Act) to hold the assets for the children until they become adults.

If your spouse had minor children who are not your children and who you have not legally adopted, and if these stepchildren have another surviving parent, that parent will almost certainly become their legal guardian even if your deceased spouse had custody of the children. The other parent will also have the right to act as conservator unless your spouse named someone else in a will to fulfill this role. Stepparents do not generally have the legal right to custody of minor stepchildren and really do not even have the right to visit them. Minor children will have the right to receive support from the decedent's estate. If any of these circumstances affect you, you should disclose them to your estate administration attorney and might also want to consult a family law attorney if you have problems or concerns in this area.

# CHAPTER 5
# GETTING FINANCIAL ADVICE

## § 5.1 Why You May Need Help

In many marriages, one spouse takes primary responsibility for financial decisions. Traditionally this was the husband, but many women are interested in finances and it is fairly common in twenty-first century marriages for the wife to be the primary financial planner, record keeper, and bill payer. It is also quite common for one spouse to take care of some financial matters and for the other spouse to take care of different ones.

If you, now a surviving spouse, were not ever interested in finances during the marriage or were not the spouse who made many financial decisions, you may feel lost without your spouse's guidance. In all honesty, you still may not be interested in learning very much about finances, although some surviving spouses do develop an interest and desire to learn once they realize how important finances are to their future quality of life. Sometimes the choice to remain ignorant about financial matters proves to be very expensive indeed. You may be so emotionally devastated that you simply are not capable of taking on the task of learning a lot of fairly complex information quickly.

Even if you are the spouse who made the financial decisions, you may not be in a good emotional state to make wise decisions, at least for a while. I have seen intelligent business people of both genders make puzzlingly foolish financial decisions soon after a spouse's death.

Widows in particular are often given a lot of free advice from friends and recommendations of various advisors by many people. We have all seen news stories in recent years about "financial advisors" who defrauded their clients and "invested" their clients' money in their own lifestyles. While the perpetrators were sent to jail, the clients' losses were not recovered because the money had been spent and the "advisor" did not have assets to attach and repay defrauded investors.

Before hiring financial expertise, it is always a good idea to interview several different financial advisors and learn as much about them and how they work as you can. If friends are recommending advisors, ask them in-depth questions about how they met the advisor, how long they have been working with him or her, the kind of services provided, the advisor's philosophy about investing, the approach the advisor took to analyzing their needs, the actual results the advisor has achieved for them, and whether or not there are minimum account sizes the advisor works with. No ethical financial advisor will guarantee you any particular return on your money. If someone is making promises that sound too good to be true, they probably are.

Be honest with yourself on the issue of whether or not you need professional financial advice and management. If you are financially inexperienced, you will likely benefit from some expert help, at least for a while, to get you started. All financial advisors are paid for their services in one form or another, so do not expect "free" advice or believe that you are getting it for free. Even mutual funds that are ordered online or by telephone without a broker charge fees.

Remember that ignorance can cost you a great deal and that good financial advisors earn their compensation by increasing your net worth, enlarging your understanding of finances, and working to diversify your assets to reduce the risk of large losses during economic downturns. Some widowed people know that they are not knowledgeable about investments but are so concerned about fees that they keep all of their money in bank certificates of deposit or in money-market funds. These vehicles have a place in people's financial lives, but keeping all of your money in these kinds of accounts practically guarantees that your asset value will not keep up with inflation over a period of years. This is not to say that you should not be cost-conscious or should spend unreasonably large amounts of money on financial advice. The prudent approach is to do some homework of your own or confer with a trusted attorney, accountant, or banker on what kind of advice and financial services would be helpful in your individual situation.

No matter what kind of advisor you ultimately choose, you should be given written information from the individual or institution on the following topics:

- The scope of services offered.
- The minimum account size the advisor will work with.

- Exactly how the advisor is compensated for services (flat fees, hourly fees, percentage of assets under management, commissions from sales of financial products), and what services are covered by the fee.

- Whether the fees are negotiable (they often are).

- How financial decisions will be made: whether the advisor (1) will have full discretion, (2) will need to consult with you on every decision, or (3) will have authority over some decisions but not others.

- The factors the advisor considers when determining a financial plan for a client. Even similarly situated clients can have different wants or needs, and a cookie-cutter approach where everyone is given the same advice is unlikely to give you the most satisfactory results.

- How the advisor will communicate with you (financial statements, periodic meetings, phone calls at will, etc.).

- The educational and professional credentials the advisor has earned, and how much experience the advisor has.

- Who will have custody of your account and who will have access to the assets (this is important for protection against financial fraud).

- Exactly who you will be working with. Many people are dissatisfied if they do not have one designated contact person to call with questions who is very familiar with their account.

- An initial, complete financial inventory and a thorough discussion about your goals; be prepared for this by having your financial inventory available and having a list of questions and issues you want to discuss. Many advisors use a financial inventory form that they will give you in advance to prepare for a first meeting. Otherwise, simply make a list of your assets and liabilities. Also make a list of the goals you are aware of.

- The flexibility of the planning. Be aware of how "locked up" your assets will be in case you need cash quickly at some time in the future. For example, some advisors routinely suggest annuities (sometimes as the only suggestion) without adequately disclosing penalties for early withdrawal, which sometimes are imposed for a number of years.

- Customer references. You should call the references and ask what they like and do not like about the advisor. What another person cares about may be very different than what matters most to you.

It is important to feel comfortable with the advisor you choose. Some people do not like to ask questions of a financial advisor because they do not want to appear ignorant, and some clients are intimidated by their advisors. A good advisor will make an effort to be sure you understand what is being discussed and recommended and encourage you to ask as many questions as you need to understand the issues fully. You are not likely to have a satisfactory relationship with good results with someone who is impatient with you or unwilling to communicate with you to the extent you want or need. Good advisors can also refer you to educational resources or can provide you with helpful reading materials. One warning, however: a warm relationship with an advisor is not enough in itself. You also need intelligent, prudent, customized advice.

## § 5.2 What Kind of Advisors Do You Want or Need?

Changes in the regulatory climate affecting investments and financial planning in recent years have blurred the old boundaries governing the type of work various financial advisors and institutions are legally permitted to perform. Banks can now offer investment services and even sell life insurance and annuities. Many CPAs offer comprehensive financial planning advice for individuals and businesses, which goes far beyond their traditional auditing and tax services. Many stock brokerages have instituted complete financial planning and management programs that can offer "one-stop shopping" for their customers. Life insurance professionals often offer complete financial planning and investment services to their clients and then to the beneficiaries of life insurance after a death.

Many of these advisors have sophisticated financial computer software that allows them to create projections for you about future values, future needs, and likely outcomes of various investment strategies. These programs are powerful tools because they allow you and your advisor to quickly and easily explore various strategies and choose the strategy that best fits your wants and needs. Many people find these kinds of financial analyses to be very enlightening and reassuring about their financial futures. There is an almost universal fear among people of all levels of wealth that they will outlive their money. This kind of financial analysis can give a realistic picture of how likely that is to happen in an individual situation. It can also let you know what kind of an income stream you can reasonably expect from investments in various likely economic scenarios, which in turn can lead to other decisions, such as whether or not to go back to work, to retire from current employment, or to sell a home in favor of a less expensive living arrangement.

The following material is a discussion of some of the kinds of financial advisors you may wish to consult and hire. Due to the ability of various kinds of professionals to provide several different types of advice and services, many people choose to hire an accountant and one other financial advisor rather than several. This is a matter of personal preference, though, and many people feel more comfortable using different professionals for specific parts of their financial needs.

## § 5.2.1 Banks and Trust Companies

Some people name a bank or trust company in a will or trust agreement to manage the estate for their surviving spouse. In other cases, a widowed person wants someone to take over his or her finances, make all the investment decisions, and help with bill paying, record keeping, and tax-return preparation. The widowed person can create his or her own revocable trust agreement and name a bank or trust company as current trustee. Bank trust departments and standalone trust companies operate within this model of financial management. Some trust departments have a lower limit on the size of trust accounts, but others are quite flexible on the size of account they will accept. Some have "packaged" programs for fairly low-cost trust arrangements appropriate for older customers and smaller accounts.

Trust department fees are typically based on a percentage of the value of the funds in trust, with the percentage going down as the size of the account increases. You should ask about financial reporting and tax-return preparation; some trust departments charge additional fees for these services. Trust departments can take over most or all bill paying and record keeping if requested. A trust department or trust company can be a good choice for a widowed person who wants very comprehensive help and does not want to make a lot of decisions on finances. However, hiring a trust department or trust company in no way means that you should thereafter ignore your finances.

If your inheritance from your spouse was placed in trust by him or her with a bank trustee, you will want to get as much information as possible from the trust officer assigned to you. You can rightfully request to deal with the same person all of the time. You should be given complete information as to the investments of the assets, the income you will receive, whether or not you have some flexibility with the trust arrangement, and any other questions you may have. Some bank trust departments invest most or all assets in proprietary bank funds from which the bank earns a profit. Some beneficiaries object to this practice. Other banks and trust companies invest in mutual funds available to the public and all kinds of publicly traded securities. You should receive clear information about how your trust assets will be invested.

If the trust your spouse left you names other people (such as children from a previous marriage) as the beneficiaries of what remains in the trust on your death (the "remainder"), the trustee will have to balance your current needs against the duty to increase the value of the trust for the benefit of the remainder beneficiaries. Financial advisors tell us that this can be a difficult task since assets that produce a lot of income typically do not increase in value as rapidly as assets that are designed to grow in value rather than produce interest or dividends.

Many widowed people are disappointed with the income they receive from this kind of trust. Some trusts, however, permit the distribution of both income and principal to a surviving spouse on a very generous basis. If your inheritance has been left to you in trust, you should have a detailed conversation with both your attorney and the trustee so that you thoroughly understand what your rights are in the trust income and principal. You should also be given all of the financial information you request as well as receiving regular statements. It is in your best interests to learn how to read the statements, even if they look confusing. Ask the trust officer to review them with you until you understand what they mean.

What can you do if you are unhappy with a bank trustee chosen by your spouse? Some trust documents permit you to remove and replace a trustee. Check with your attorney on this issue. If the trust document permits you to remove and replace the trustee, you can interview several banks and trust companies and choose one with which you are more comfortable. Many trust documents, however, do not permit removal of a trustee. Sometimes a deceased spouse was concerned with preserving assets so that they would last for the surviving spouse's lifetime and then be passed on to children. This feels too controlling to some surviving spouses or comes as a shock. If you are very unhappy with this kind of arrangement, consult with your attorney to determine your options.

Banks are also now allowed by law to give investment advice outside of their trust departments. Some banks have separate departments created to fulfill this function for bank customers, rather like an in-house stock brokerage. You could, therefore, turn over investment management to a bank without actually creating a trust. Many banks are working to become total financial resources for their customers.

## § 5.2.2 Accountants and Bookkeepers; Taxes and Record Keeping

Despite the notorious accounting and financial business scandals of recent years, individuals often develop a great deal of trust in their accountants. Accountants are viewed by the general public as careful, conservative, and trustworthy. In part, I believe that this is because they are not compensated in any way that would induce them to give advice to their clients that would result in a financial benefit to themselves (such as a commission payment arrangement). They are simply paid cash for their time and advice. Money is also a very intimate and private subject in American culture; many people are more private about their finances than any other aspect of their lives. Since people must talk frankly to their accountants about finances, they often feel a greater level of trust and intimacy with an accountant than with other professionals who provide advice to them.

Most individuals become familiar with accountants initially because they need help with tax-return preparation and personal income tax planning. Even if you have not used an accountant for these reasons in the past, it is probably advisable to consult one for the first couple of years after a spouse's death, since some tax issues arise only in the context of a death and you are unlikely to be aware of them on your own.

Traditionally, accountants were not trained—or expected—to offer investment advice. Now, however, many accountants who work with individuals offer comprehensive financial planning and refer their clients to other advisors, such as stockbrokers, insurance professionals, and real estate brokers. Accountants often have a more detailed and thorough understanding of financial issues than any other advisor. I believe that a skilled and ethical accountant is a crucially important advisor in practically everyone's life. An accountant may or may not be the best investment advisor, but accountants who do not offer investment advice will likely be able to direct you to a source of advice or services whose work they have reviewed and in whom they have developed confidence.

Many accountants have bookkeepers on staff or who they can refer their clients to. If you are not familiar with financial record keeping or simply do not want to take on the task for yourself, you might consider hiring a professional bookkeeper, at least for a while, to help you set up a workable and appropriate system. Bookkeepers typically have accounting education and skills without having become certified public accountants. Certified public accountants must pass a series of national examinations to become "certified" and participate in annual continuing education to keep their certification.

Increasingly, people are using computers, and various software companies have developed bookkeeping and accounting programs designed for individuals (as distinguished from businesses). Quicken is probably the best-known, and many people find that using this software is adequate for their financial record-keeping needs. An accountant could also suggest software you might want to try.

It is very important to your financial future to be sure that you have a good financial tax and bookkeeping system in place. Your situation may be simple enough that you do not need long-term help, and you may be able to handle most matters yourself, but you can avoid many financial and tax mistakes by getting help early on.

### § 5.2.3 Stockbrokers: What Is Their Role?

Stockbrokers sell stocks, bonds, mutual funds—essentially securities of all kinds. Some focus on certain kinds of investments. Stockbrokers are highly regulated by federal and state law, and must pass certain licensing examinations. Some people who work in stock brokerages are "registered investment advisors" who have a fiduciary duty to their customers to put the customers' best interests before their own. This is a much greater advisory role than a traditional brokerage function; brokers merely have to advise their customers about a particular investment's suitability for them. You should be given a clear statement as to whether or not a stockbroker is acting as a fiduciary on your behalf.

Brokers typically are paid a commission of a percentage of the cost of the assets bought or sold, although many now have customer arrangements where they are paid an annual fee based on a percentage of the value of the accounts they manage. Customers are increasingly requesting the option to pay a percentage rather than commissions because their costs are more predictable. The drawback to straight commission compensation is that the broker may be tempted to suggest more trading than might be in the customer's best interest just to increase his or her own income. The drawback to a compensation system based on the value of the account is that the broker may be tempted to invest for growth rather than income, which might not be the best strategy for a particular customer. The broker might also counsel customers against doing anything to reduce the value of the account, such as liquidating assets to pay off debt, even if this would be in the customer's best interest. There is no perfect system that fits every customer, so it is important to analyze your own needs and work with a broker or advisor who will maximize the benefit to you under either system.

Stockbrokers often work in large national firms. Many others, however, affiliate with smaller local or regional firms. I have seen excellent results for clients in both environments. I have also seen poor ones in all kinds of firms.

Many brokerage firms that offer registered investment advisory services have now developed sophisticated programs for their customers, which provide comprehensive financial planning that can be very helpful to clients. If you choose to work with a registered investment advisor, I would recommend that you at least give him or her enough information about your total financial situation so that the advisor can design an investment program that meshes with the rest of your financial life.

Make sure you clearly understand whether or not the advisor will take any investment action without discussing it with you in advance. Generally, a broker will make a recommendation to you but will not take action without your consent. Some customers give their brokers or advisors authority to make some decisions without discussing it with them in advance.

Stockbrokers and registered investment advisors have no control over the stock market and are not responsible for market problems, such as what we have seen since 2000. Good ones, however, can design a diversified portfolio that is not too concentrated in any one sector of the economy and can keep a close watch on investments and act to minimize losses.

## § 5.2.4 Money Managers

The term "money manager" can describe anyone from a sophisticated Wall Street firm that manages investments for large pension plans and insurance companies to an individual who manages investments for other individuals. They are typically paid a percentage of the value of the funds under their management. Money managers develop a written investment plan with their customers and are given authority by the customer to make investments that fall within the goals of the plan. The term "money manager" is a discretionary description (unlike, for example, "certified public accountant," which is a regulated title requiring certain credentials).

## § 5.2.5 Financial Planners

The term "financial planner" is not strictly regulated and can encompass professionals in a number of areas with varying professional licenses and qualifications. In my experience, people in a wide range of financial services call themselves "financial planners." They typically fall into two general categories:

Fee-based independent planners who charge an hourly fee or periodic retainer for their services and do not sell any investment or financial products.

Planners who receive commission sale compensation for selling financial products.

True hourly-rate financial planners are fairly rare unless they are also CPAs. Many people trust them since they are compensated only for their time and knowledge and have no self-interest in the advice they give. In other words, they are not paid more or less for suggesting certain products or strategies.

Many professionals in the insurance and annuity industries call themselves financial planners. Financial planners from various disciplines can offer excellent advice. It is in your best interest, however, to be very clear on how they are compensated and for them to give you complete information on their educational and professional credentials, experience, and any special expertise they may have in certain areas.

## § 5.2.6 Life Insurance Professionals

If you are the beneficiary of life insurance from your deceased spouse, the insurance professional who handled your spouse's insurance planning may also be able to provide financial services to you now. Many insurance companies also offer investment products and services. Many experienced insurance professionals also have securities licenses and years of experience helping clients with comprehensive personal and business financial planning. If you have dependents, you should discuss the need to acquire life insurance on your own life to protect them. As with any advisor, an insurance professional should take a complete financial inventory of your assets, liabilities, and needs and provide you with a diversified plan to meet your goals.

## § 5.3 Working with Your Team

You may assemble your team by accepting the referral of professionals recommended to you by a trusted accountant or attorney or you may choose your advisors from other referral sources. I am convinced, however, that your financial "team members" need to know about each other, and all of them need to clearly understand your needs, goals, and strategies so that they can work together to accomplish them. You may want to request a meeting where all of your advisors are present with you and your financial issues can be discussed so the advisors can offer suggestions to create a comprehensive plan for your benefit. You may wish to have this kind of meeting on an annual or more frequent basis to be sure things are progressing as you want them to. You can request meetings with any of your financial advisors on a regular basis. Some very conscientious financial advisors have a policy that they meet with all of their clients quarterly or semiannually. They review the status of the work they are doing for their clients and discuss with them any issues that have arisen that would indicate a need for a change.

I have had the benefit of being able to observe my clients' experiences with different financial professionals and different strategies over the years without having personal financial risk. I have seen all of the different kinds of advisors achieve good results for clients in various contexts. I have also seen advisors who take advantage of unsophisticated clients and who give advice designed to enrich themselves at the expense of their clients. There are competent, intelligent, experienced, and ethical advisors available to the public; if you need help, they are the ones to choose.

# CHAPTER 6
# ESTATE ADMINISTRATION

## § 6.1 The Purpose of the Process

The purpose of the estate administration process is to transfer ownership of a decedent's assets to the people who are entitled to receive them. The right to the decedent's property can arise under a will, by the laws of intestacy, by contract, or by means of joint tenancy with right of survivorship. It can also arise because the decedent owed a person money under a variety of circumstances. This chapter will discuss various methods of transferring property.

Many people interpret the term "property" to refer only to real estate; but for purposes of this book, the term refers to anything of value. Property includes bank accounts, investments (such as stocks and bonds), privately owned businesses, household goods, jewelry, vehicles, sporting equipment, and more unusual assets like patents, oil and gas rights, the right to proceeds from a lawsuit, the right to payment of debts owed to a decedent, and anything else of value.

Anything a deceased person owned in his or her sole name is likely to be subject to the probate process. Attorneys refer to these assets as "probate assets" because they cannot be transferred to the heirs without going through probate. Probate is the legal process of court-approved transfer of title to a decedent's assets. If the decedent had a will, the probate will be referred to as "testate" (the legal term for the estate of a person who died with a will). If the decedent did not have a will, the probate estate is referred to as "intestate." All states have statutes that determine who inherits from a person who died without a will. These statutes are referred to as "intestacy statutes."

Colorado has adopted the Uniform Probate Code, which provides for a simplified probate procedure through the courts. The vast majority of Colorado probate cases do not require anyone to appear in court. A formal process, which does require court hearings, is available if a party requests it in specific circumstances. The formal process is considerably more expensive, and the person requesting it may be required to pay the additional costs.

Probate cases are filed in the state district court for the county where the decedent died. Denver County has the only dedicated probate court with a permanent probate judge in Colorado, and Denver probate cases are filed in that court. If there are concerns about the handling of an estate, it is possible to petition the court to "supervise" a probate proceeding. The court may also be petitioned to require that the Personal Representative post a bond to protect the value of the estate from any losses or wrongdoing.

If there was a will, the language of the document should describe what is to happen to all of the probate assets. If there was not a will, the intestacy statute determines who will inherit from the probate estate. In Colorado intestate estates, surviving spouses inherit a percentage of the probate estate based on a number of factors, including whether or not there were children from the marriage, the age of those children, and whether or not the decedent's parents also survived him or her.

# § 6.2 First Steps

## § 6.2.1 Be Sure You Are a Surviving Spouse

Colorado and some other states recognize common law marriage. A common law marriage is established by the husband and wife "holding themselves out" as married. In other words, they cause other people to believe that they are married by their words and actions. If you were married in a ceremony and with a license in any state, you should not have problems establishing that you are now a surviving spouse, although you may need to produce a copy of your marriage certificate for some purposes, such as Social Security claims. If you and your deceased spouse were not married in a ceremony with a license, but lived as husband and wife, you likely do have legal rights as a spouse, but you may have more difficulty with the process. You may need the assistance of an attorney who practices in the area of family law to help you enforce your rights as a surviving spouse.

## § 6.2.2 Determine Domicile

Domicile is the legal concept of where a person legally resided and which state has jurisdiction over the probate process. The state of domicile will also have an impact on taxes. Each person has only one domicile. Sometimes it is difficult to determine where it is, though.

There is no one factor that definitively determines domicile. Factors to be considered include:

1. Where the decedent voted;

2. Where the decedent registered vehicles and had a driver's license;

3. Where the decedent stated residence on tax returns and paid state income tax;

4. Where the decedent's largest residence is located;

5. Where the decedent worked, had a professional license, or owned a business;

6. Where the decedent belonged to social, charitable, and religious organizations;

7. Where the decedent spent most of his or her time; and

8. Where the decedent stated he or she lived in the will.

Obviously, any of these factors can change over time. Many retired people spend winters in warm states and the rest of the year in their "home" state without intending to become permanent residents of the warm-weather state. Other people own or rent vacation homes in several different parts of the country or own investment real estate in more than one state and spend varying amounts of time in several states in different years. Domicile is not always simple to determine and can be very important to the outcome of some estates.

It is essential, however, to make a determination of one state as the domicile. The principal administration activities will take place under the legal structure of that state. The attorney primarily responsible for the administration of the estate should be located in the state of domicile. If the decedent owned real estate in other states, it will probably be necessary to open an "ancillary" probate in each of those states to deal with the real estate. Intangible assets, such as stocks, bonds, insurance, and retirement plans, are considered to be located in the domicile state of a decedent. Real estate, in contrast, is actually physically located in a specific place and is subject to the laws of that jurisdiction. Ancillary probate is usually a simplified and abbreviated process that only deals with the property in the ancillary state. It will probably be necessary to engage an attorney who practices in the ancillary state as well as an attorney in the state of domicile. This book refers to Colorado state law on issues of probate administration, but many of the concepts are similar in other states.

## § 6.2.3 Collect Asset Information and Determine If Probate Is Necessary

The first step in the administration process is to collect complete information as to everything your spouse owned or had any legal rights to. This includes real estate, bank accounts, retirement plans and IRAs, life insurance, stocks, bonds, mutual funds, privately held businesses, and promissory notes—in short, anything of any value.

The next step is to determine how the assets were owned and if they have beneficiary designations. Anything you and your spouse owned as joint tenants with right of survivorship will pass to you outside of the probate process. Anything your spouse owned with any other person as joint tenants with right of survivorship will pass to the other joint tenant(s) outside of the probate process. Anything your spouse owned that had a valid beneficiary designation will pass to the beneficiary outside of the probate process, with some exceptions discussed below. Assets your spouse owned in his or her sole name will likely need to be transferred through the probate process, unless the total value of the estate is no more than $50,000 and no real estate is involved. In that case, a form of simplified small estate administration is possible using some standardized forms.

## § 6.2.4 Secure Assets

You may need to take immediate steps to safeguard assets. This is particularly important with vacant real estate and businesses. As difficult as it may be to think about this at such an emotional time, someone must take steps to protect the real estate from intruders and to run the business "as usual." I have had experiences where relatives descended on the home and helped themselves to personal items without permission. This is improper and should be prevented by having someone stay at the home to safeguard its contents.

People often state that the decedent "promised" them certain items, but until it is determined whether or not this was stated in a will or memorandum of disposition of personal property, and prior to an appraisal, nothing should be disposed of.

## § 6.2.5 Determine If There Is a Will or Living Trust

Every effort should be made to determine if there is a will or living trust created by the decedent. This is not always easy. If you know that your spouse had these instruments, you may likely know where they are located. If not, try to determine whether or not your spouse had an attorney and ask the attorney if he or she knows whether there is a will or trust (and where the original documents are located). You could also inquire at your spouse's bank to see if he or she had a safe deposit box. Sometimes it is necessary to contact several banks to locate the safe deposit box. In Colorado, unlike in some other states, a bank will allow a safe deposit box to be opened in the presence of a bank officer for the purpose of finding a will.

A surprising number of people keep original wills and trusts in drawers in their home or office. In my experience, families have found wills packed away in boxes in storage facilities, stored in attics, kept in trunks with military memorabilia, and folded in Bibles. If you find a photocopy of a will or trust, but not the original, the copy may give you some clues as to where to look for the original, such as the name of the attorney who prepared it. Some law firms habitually keep original wills and send copies to their clients stating that the original is kept at the law firm. In that case, you can make a simple phone call to locate the original.

If you cannot find the original will, it may have been revoked or it may simply be lost. There is a presumption in the law that if the original will cannot be found, the decedent revoked it. But this is just a presumption, and can be overcome. It is sometimes possible to administer an estate using a photocopy of a will, but this is more difficult than using an original. Consult with your attorney on how to proceed, because in some cases the result from an intestate probate would not be much different than what would happen under the lost will. In other cases, it will be very different and well worth the time and effort to locate the will.

Colorado and some other states recognize holographic wills. These are handwritten wills that must be written and signed by the decedent. They can be admitted to probate and used to administer an estate. A printed form will is not a holographic will since it is not all in the decedent's handwriting. A printed form will needs to be signed in the presence of a notary and two witnesses, while a holographic will needs only the decedent's signature. I have been asked several times during the last few years if a computerized form will that was found on a decedent's computer but was never printed or signed is a valid will. It is not.

If no will or trust can be found, and you determine that it is necessary or desirable to open probate, you can proceed to do so under the intestacy statute. If a will is found later, the form of probate can be changed to deal with the will.

## § 6.2.6 Determine the Value of the Estate

The next preliminary step is to determine the value of these assets. The value must be determined as of the date of death. Some assets are easy to value; for example, banks can provide accurate information as to the balance of an account on any given day. Life insurance companies can give an accurate statement (called a Form 712) of the death benefit, outstanding loans against the policy, and interest paid on the policy from the date of death until the date the benefits were paid. Brokers can provide the value of publicly traded stocks and bonds, although they need to be advised to use the valuation method required by the IRS.

Real estate needs to be appraised by a qualified appraiser who is familiar with the IRS requirements for estate tax appraisals. Taxing authorities do not accept appraisals prepared by lenders, nor do they accept the county tax assessor's valuation. Privately owned businesses need to be appraised by a qualified business appraiser. These appraisals can be prepared with different approaches that have enormous impact on the future of the business and the family and need to be prepared by appraisers who thoroughly understand the tax and legal ramifications of their work. Appraisers can arrive at significantly different values for privately owned businesses by focusing on different factors impacting the business. The value of the business is of great importance to the family of the business owner, any business partners, potential buyers, the IRS, and creditors of the business or the decedent. Jewelry, art, and household goods should be appraised by appraisers who specialize in these areas.

Appraisals are extremely important for a number of reasons. Inherited assets receive a new date-of-death value tax cost basis that will determine the capital gain tax paid when assets are later sold. The Personal Representative needs appraised values of all the estate assets in order to accurately distribute the estate to the heirs and beneficiaries in the percentages stated in the will or the intestacy statute. The IRS and state taxing authorities will base estate and inheritance taxes on the appraised value of the estate assets. Appraisals may be necessary to comply with contracts with co-owners of a business that require the purchase of the interest of a deceased owner of the business by the surviving owners.

## § 6.3 Opening Probate and Appointing the Personal Representative

### § 6.3.1 The Role of the Personal Representative

The Personal Representative is the person either named in a will or who has priority under the intestacy statute to administer the probate estate. In cases where there is no will, the intestacy statute lists persons with priority for appointment as Personal Representative in descending order, starting with a surviving spouse. A Personal Representative must be appointed in writing by the court before he or she can take action as Personal Representative. An application must be sent to the court along with several other documents; if it is approved by the court, a document called "Letters Testamentary" or "Letters of Administration" will be issued. These Letters are evidence of the legal authority of the Personal Representative to take action on behalf of the estate.

In some states, a Personal Representative is called an executor or executrix, but "Personal Representative" is the proper legal term in Colorado. There can be more than one Personal Representative acting at the same time. The Personal Representative does not have to be an individual; banks, trust companies, and law firms are often appointed as Personal Representative in wills or by agreement between the heirs. A professional Personal Representative can offer skilled services and can act effectively in cases where there is family conflict. If other family members have feelings of distrust or antipathy toward the Personal Representative named in the will or the person with priority for appointment, an agreement to appoint a professional to act in that capacity can reassure everyone that the Personal Representative will not favor any beneficiary over any other and will not hide information.

## § 6.3.2 Do You Want to Serve as Personal Representative?

Even if you are named in your spouse's will or if you have priority for court appointment as a surviving spouse, you do not have to accept an appointment as Personal Representative if you do not want to. Many wills have successors named to act in this capacity if the surviving spouse does not want to act or cannot act for any reason. The intestacy statute has alternatives with lower priority than spouses.

Serving as Personal Representative can be tedious and time consuming. Personal Representatives also open themselves to personal liability for failing to act properly and in the best interest of all of the beneficiaries. This means not favoring themselves over other beneficiaries or enriching themselves at the expense of the other beneficiaries. It means making good business decisions regarding assets and getting appropriate professional advice to assist in this process. It means keeping the beneficiaries adequately informed about what is going on in the estate. It means keeping very accurate books and records or hiring someone to perform this function. All of these obligations (and more) are part of what is called "fiduciary duty." In addition to all of their other duties, Personal Representatives are personally liable for any unpaid taxes owed by the estate. Sometimes a surviving spouse views all of these duties as too much of a burden and prefers that someone else act instead.

Most surviving spouses, however, very much want to serve as Personal Representative because they want to control the process and guide it as much as possible. There are usually some decisions to be made—with several choices available—that will impact the surviving spouse's life, and he or she would like the opportunity to make those decisions. It is also a way to become educated financially, which is of future benefit provided that the spouse gets adequate professional help in conducting the process properly. Just because you have never had any experience in estate administration or do not have a business career, it does not follow that you are not competent to serve as Personal Representative. As long as you are willing to get good professional advice and take care to act ethically, your lack of experience should not be a reason not to serve.

The decision about whether or not to serve as Personal Representative of a deceased spouse's estate is very personal. Problems often arise, however, if the surviving spouse is not in good enough health physically or mentally to properly manage the estate or when the spouse is not receiving competent professional advice. It can be a daunting and time-consuming job, so be honest with yourself about whether it is the right thing for you.

One factor in your analysis needs to be the issue of who would serve if you do not. If you want a professional Personal Representative (such as a bank) to serve and none is named in the will, the heirs and beneficiaries will need to agree to appoint one, and sometimes it is not possible to get agreement. If the person who would serve in your place is someone you trust, the choice to renounce your right to serve will be easier.

Another very important factor in making this decision is whether or not you are the sole beneficiary of the estate. If you are, the process may be much simpler since no one else's rights and welfare are involved.

## § 6.3.3 What If Someone Else Is Named as Personal Representative in the Will?

It used to be very common for husbands to appoint a bank, attorney, business partner, son, or other male relative as Personal Representative in wills, under the assumption that women could not take on the burden of serving or would not be financially sophisticated enough to do a competent job. This attitude is far less common now and is less common in certain parts of the country than others. Most of the wills I see for married people which are prepared in Colorado name the spouse (of either gender) as the first nominee for Personal Representative.

With second marriages and premarital agreements becoming more common, however, many people name someone other than a spouse as Personal Representative. Sometimes this is because the spouses waive their rights to inherit from each other in a premarital agreement and all of the assets are going to pass to the children. Sometimes a bank or other corporate fiduciary is named as Personal Representative to avoid conflict between a spouse and stepchildren. Sometimes a decedent prepared a will prior to a marriage and named a sibling or someone else as Personal Representative and then never got around to changing it. If an old will names a former spouse, that appointment will be invalid under the law. Other appointments in wills signed before the marriage may be upheld on challenge.

If someone is appointed in your spouse's will and you genuinely object to that appointment, consult an attorney as soon as possible to determine what your rights may be to remove that person. If a bank or trust company is named, it will be quite difficult to remove them since they are presumably competent and impartial. Be aware, however, that as a beneficiary of an estate, you have significant rights to obtain information about everything that goes on throughout the process. Even if you are not going to serve as Personal Representative, you might be well advised to consult with an attorney of your own to advise you as a beneficiary and to make sure your rights are protected.

Surviving spouses are sometimes disappointed to learn that what they are to receive from their deceased spouse's estate is going to be held in a trust with someone else as trustee and that they are never going to gain absolute control over it. I see this happen in cases where one spouse is not very experienced handling money and the deceased spouse wanted to provide for professional management to make sure the assets last as long as possible for the protection of the surviving spouse. Sometimes the decedent wanted to make sure that the family assets eventually pass to the children, rather than to a subsequent spouse of the widowed person. Sometimes a deceased spouse feared that the widowed person would be victimized by "gold diggers" who would marry them for their money and wanted to protect against that possibility. If your inheritance has been left in trust and you do not understand all the reasons for this arrangement or do not like it, consult with an attorney who will represent you personally and advise you as to what options you may have to overturn this arrangement.

## § 6.3.4 Bond

Personal Representatives are sometimes required to purchase a bond from an insurance company to protect the value of the estate. Wills typically waive this requirement in writing. If you are required to post bond, try to avoid taking any action as Personal Representative until the bond is issued. If you are not the Personal Representative, you may want whoever is serving to be bonded for your protection. Discuss questions on bonding with your attorney.

### § 6.3.5 Determine Heirs

If your spouse's estate is intestate (*i.e.*, there was no will), it is necessary to determine the heirs. Heirs are the people who inherit under the law. Colorado's intestacy statute sets out specifically who inherits from a person who has died without a will. Surviving spouses sometimes, but not always, inherit the entire estate. It is quite common that children of prior marriages or even surviving parents inherit a part of an intestate estate. It is crucial to work through this issue with your attorney so you can properly notify the heirs and deal with any uncertainty as to the identity of the heirs. It is sometimes necessary to go so far as to hire a private investigator to locate heirs with whom the decedent was not in recent contact. I have had cases where a surviving spouse discovered only after death that the decedent had children from a prior relationship.

## § 6.4 Exempt Property and Family Allowance

In addition to what you inherit from your spouse, you and your dependent children are entitled to an additional amount from the estate called an exempt property allowance and a family allowance in amounts up to $50,000. You will not receive these allowances automatically and will need to apply for them by filing a claim in the court and with the Personal Representative. There are tax and other ramifications that go along with these allowances and they are not necessarily the right choice in all cases, so consult with your attorney about this issue. For example, if you are the sole heir or beneficiary of an estate, there may be no point in requesting these allowances unless your spouse left significant debt.

## § 6.5 Debts

Debts owed by a decedent become claims against that person's estate after death. Most estates have some debts because most people have some debt, even if it is just medical bills for the final illness. In some cases the debt is minor in comparison with the value of the estate, but in others the debt balance is larger than the value of the estate. These estates are referred to as "insolvent estates" and the probate code provides a priority list of which creditors get paid in what order if the estate is insolvent.

There are two basic kinds of debts in estates: known and unknown. These debts can be either secured or unsecured. Secured debt has collateral pledged to ensure payment. The most common example of secured debt is a home mortgage. If the homeowner fails to make the payments, the lender can start a foreclosure proceeding and take ownership of the house and sell it to someone else. Car loans are typically secured by the vehicle, and the lender can repossess the car if the debt is not paid.

Unsecured debts have no collateral pledged against them. Examples of unsecured debt are most credit card debt, medical bills, and the like. Secured lenders retain their rights under the security arrangement that originally secured the debt. For example, a mortgage lender retains the right to foreclose on a defaulted home loan regardless of the death of the borrower.

It is very important for the Personal Representative of an estate to determine accurately what the debts of the decedent are before dispensing money to a beneficiary or even before paying any but the most essential bills. Paying some creditors and not paying others, which is giving some creditors preference, can open the Personal Representative to personal liability.

## § 6.5.1 Determine What the Debts Are

Some debts will become obvious fairly soon when bills come in the mail. Other debts are considered "known" because the Personal Representative has or "should have" actual knowledge of them. For example, if the decedent was hospitalized or spent time in a nursing home or rehabilitation center, there will obviously be bills from the facilities and from doctors. The law takes the position that the Personal Representative knew these facts even if he or she has not received actual notice from the creditors. Other debts may come as a surprise. Some people keep secrets from their spouses and some of those secrets involve debt.

## § 6.5.2 The Claims Process and "Surprise" Debt

There is a statutory process for handling claims against an estate. Most claims against an estate must be made within one year of the decedent's death or they are forever barred. There are some exceptions to this rule. The claims period can be shortened even further by publishing notice in the newspaper that a person has died and giving the contact information to make a claim against the estate. If the Personal Representative does this, the period for making claims can be shortened to four months after the date it was first published. Claims made within that time period can be denied (only for good reason) if done within 60 days after the claims period. Many claims made after this period can be denied. There is often controversy if a claim is denied and the creditor claims that the debt was "known" but the Personal Representative argues that it was not.

In general, most estate debts must be paid, but there are some that may not have to be. If a claim was truly "unknown" and is presented after one year or the end of the claims period after publication of notice, it can be denied. If you deny payment, expect possible legal action from the creditor to compel payment. If the estate is insolvent, many creditors simply accept that they will not be paid. If the debt was truly a separate debt of the decedent, a surviving spouse will not be liable for payment. But if the spouse also is a co-debtor (for example, on joint credit cards), then the surviving spouse will remain liable for payment. Some creditors argue that any debt of a married person is actually the debt of both spouses.

Many married couples are jointly obligated on all loans incurred by either of them. There are some unusual forms of debt, however, that may not be joint. For example, one spouse might personally guarantee a business loan without the other spouse's knowledge. Estate debt can become a very complex matter—so if an unknown debt appears, consult your attorney to find out whether it must be paid and by whom.

If an estate is insolvent, some of the debt will never be paid. It is important, however, to work with your attorney to make sure the debts are paid properly and in the order required by statute. If debts remain unpaid, you may face legal action by creditors who want to prove that the debt was yours as well as your deceased spouse's.

Occasionally, a surviving spouse discovers that the deceased spouse had incurred large credit card debts or mortgaged the home or had significant business debts the surviving spouse had no knowledge of. If these debts will cause a serious problem for the survivor, he or she should consult legal counsel. In some cases, creditors will accept reduced payments, but in others you may have to consider bankruptcy.

## § 6.5.3 Exempt Assets

Some assets are exempt from the reach of your spouse's creditors. These include qualified retirement plans and IRAs (in Colorado). There is some legal authority that joint tenancy property is exempt from the creditors of a deceased joint tenant. Life insurance benefits that pass to an individual (rather than to the estate itself) are the property of the beneficiary. Assets held in certain kinds of trusts are not available to creditors. Because certain assets may be legally protected, you should not use them immediately to pay creditors when bills come in.

## § 6.5.4 Notifying Creditors

The Personal Representative should notify known creditors that the decedent has died. In particular, credit card companies should be notified immediately when someone dies, to prevent wrongful use of the cards and identity theft. I recommend that one of the credit reporting bureaus (Experian, TransUnion, or Equifax) also be notified of the death to avoid identity theft and financial fraud. Under federal law, a surviving spouse does not have to refinance a mortgage after the death of a spouse or requalify for a mortgage loan. You can continue to live in your home as long as you continue to make the mortgage payments on time.

## § 6.5.5 Tax Identification Number and Accounting System

The estate will need to apply to the IRS for a separate federal tax identification number and report all financial events, income, and expenses using that number until the administration process is completed and all taxes paid, claims paid, and assets distributed to the beneficiaries. It is essential to set up a complete and accurate accounting system to keep track of all the estate's income and expenditures.

### § 6.5.6 Paying the Estate's Bills

An estate should have its own checking account, in the name of the estate, with the estate's federal tax identification number (*not* the Social Security number of the decedent or the Personal Representative). All estate expenses should be paid from this one account. Very careful records must be kept of everything that comes into the estate and of all of the expenses paid from the estate. Do not co-mingle your personal funds with this account. Do not pay estate bills from your personal checking account, nor pay your personal expenses from the estate checking account.

## § 6.6 Estate Tax Returns and Taxes

The United States has had an estate tax system since 1916. The term "estate tax" refers to the tax levied at the death of certain taxpayers based on the value of their "taxable estates." Congress significantly changed the law on estate tax in 2001. Under current law, the estate tax is scheduled to be repealed in 2010 (for that year only) and will return in 2011. Estate tax has the highest rates of any form of tax in this country—37 percent to 48 percent as of 2005. Less than two percent of estates need to file a federal estate tax return, but you must find out if your spouse's estate is required to. A filing requirement does not necessarily mean that tax will be due.

### § 6.6.1 Which Estates Must File Estate Tax Returns

The estate of any decedent whose taxable estate is more than $1,500,000 (in 2005) in total gross value must file a federal estate tax return. The dollar amount over which a return is required is scheduled to change in 2006 and later in the decade. In many states, if a federal estate tax return is required, then a state estate or inheritance tax return is required as well. As of January 1, 2005, Colorado no longer imposes a state estate tax. If the decedent owned real estate in other states, state estate tax returns will need to be filed in those states too.

The value of a taxable estate includes everything the decedent owned or had any rights to, valued at the decedent's date of death. This includes life insurance (to the extent of the death benefit, not the cash value). Many people know that life insurance is not taxed as income, but most are unaware that it is subject to estate tax. The accuracy of appraisals is obviously very important in determining whether an estate has to file a return at all and how much tax will be due. In some cases, the gross value of a decedent's taxable estate is more than $1.5 million, but the debts are significant and the net value of the estate is far lower. Even if this is the case, an estate tax return must be filed by any estate with assets worth more than $1.5 million.

In many cases where a decedent is survived by a spouse, there is no estate tax owed even if a return is required, due to the unlimited tax deduction allowed for bequests to surviving spouses. This may not be the case for every surviving spouse, though. In order to qualify for this unlimited tax deduction, property must pass to the surviving spouse in specific ways. Anything that passes outright to the spouse qualifies for the unlimited marital deduction, but assets passing through trusts may or may not qualify, depending on the terms of the trust.

Estate tax returns are typically prepared by the attorney who administers the estate or by an accountant. Not all accountants prepare estate tax returns, although some do. Some attorneys also do not prepare these returns. Estate tax returns are very important in estates, so raise this issue early with your estate administration attorney if he or she does not raise it with you.

## § 6.6.2 Deadlines for Filing Returns and Qualified Disclaimers

Federal estate tax returns are due nine months after the decedent's date of death. An automatic six-month extension is available if it is applied for before the return is past due.

If a qualified disclaimer is advisable, it is due no later than nine months after the date of death. Qualified disclaimers are written statements that a beneficiary or heir refuses to accept property from an estate. Disclaimers are most often advised for tax reasons or because a beneficiary would rather have the property pass to his or her children than accept it. Disclaimers can take several different forms, depending on what kind of asset is being disclaimed. They must be sent to the court and to different institutions, also depending on the nature of the asset. It is possible to disclaim most kinds of assets, including joint tenancy property of all kinds, life insurance, retirement plans, and real estate. In order for a disclaimer to be effective, it is crucial that you do not "accept" any benefit of the asset prior to your disclaimer. Disclaimers can be very technical and are usually made at the suggestion of a tax advisor. They can provide significant tax benefits to a family, so be sure to ask your advisors if a disclaimer might be useful in your situation, and do not rush to retitle all of your spouse's assets into your own name without considering this issue.

### § 6.6.3 Payment of Estate Tax

Estate tax is due in cash nine months after the decedent's death, even if an extension of time for filing the return has been granted. In some cases, this poses a great hardship because the estate holds little or no cash. Some estates have great value subject to estate tax, but consist of illiquid assets such as real estate or closely held businesses. If it becomes apparent that your spouse's estate owes tax and does not have the cash to pay it, start working with your attorney and accountant as soon as possible to deal with this issue. In some cases, the estate can enter into a payment plan for the taxes. Sometimes estates are able to borrow money from banks or other lenders to pay the tax.

If you are fortunate, your spouse will have left you adequate funds in a manner that qualifies for the estate tax marital deduction and no tax will be due. It is important for you to do your own estate planning, however, to avoid creating a liquidity problem for your children at your own death.

### § 6.6.4 Estate Income Tax

After a person dies, his or her estate becomes a separate taxpayer. Like other taxpayers, estates have to pay income tax, both federal and state, on income earned by the estate. Tax-exempt income from investments such as municipal bonds is tax-exempt for an estate just as it is for an individual.

Unfortunately, the income tax rates for estates and trusts are different than they are for individuals. Estates and trusts that retain income must pay the income tax at these higher rates. If, on the other hand, the income from the trust or estate is distributed to the beneficiaries during the year, the individuals will pay the tax at their own rates, which are usually lower than the rates for the estate or trust.

Estates do not have to operate on a calendar year, and many estate administration attorneys recommend using a fiscal (non-calendar) year for the estate.

If your attorney does not address the issue of estate income tax with you early in the process, be sure to ask about it.

You will also need to file a final federal and state income tax return for your spouse, for the portion of the year prior to his or her death. You can file this return jointly if you wish.

## § 6.7 What If Your Spouse Owned a Business?

If your spouse owned a private business, either alone or with other business-owner partners, you will be faced with greater complexity than many other surviving spouses. A privately owned business is one whose stock is not sold to the general public. Privately held businesses are very common and are a large economic factor in this country. I see more conflict and problems after the death of business owners than in most other cases. This discussion applies to all forms of privately held businesses, whether sole proprietorships, corporations, limited liability companies (LLCs), or partnerships. In many cases, unfortunately, a private business is something that must be dealt with quickly after a death, at a time when a surviving spouse feels least able to take on such a daunting project. But if a business is not attended to, then significant problems can arise and an asset that could provide value for the family (i.e., the business) simply loses its value for lack of immediate attention.

The first step in analyzing what to do with the business is to determine exactly what your spouse owned. In other words, what kind of a legal entity is the business, and how much of it did your spouse own? If your spouse owned 100 percent of the business, you are likely to be in sole control of what happens to it. If he or she owned less than 100 percent but more than 50 percent of the business, you will still be in control, but your control will be subject to the rights of the other owners.

The second step in dealing with a private business is to determine if there are any kinds of buy-sell arrangements in place, which govern what happens if a business owner dies. These agreements are quite common in situations where there are multiple business owners. They are by no means universal, however. Buy-sell agreements are extremely important, and I cannot overemphasize how many problems they can help avoid. I recommend that everyone who owns any interest in a private business with other people have a good agreement in place as to what the business owners would want to have happen if one of them were to die.

The third step is to determine the value of the business. If there is a buy-sell agreement in place, it likely has a method for determining the value of a deceased owner's interest in the business. However, you may not agree with the value under the agreement. Be aware that if your spouse was a business owner, you need the advice of both an attorney who deals in business continuity issues and a sophisticated business accountant.

## § 6.7.1 Continuing to Operate the Business

If you were involved in the business with your spouse, you may be able to continue to run it yourself. Or, if there are other owners, they may be able to continue the business operations. There may be key employees who could operate the business for you. It is likely, however, that there will be some disruption in running the business even if there are other owners or key employees. This issue should be explored as soon as possible and discussed fully and honestly with other owners and/or key employees to determine if it is possible to continue operations, at least for a while. Some businesses buy so-called "key man" or "key person" life insurance to provide the business with cash to help with loss of revenue or the need to hire new employees when a business owner dies. You should find out if your spouse's business has this kind of insurance and who the owner and beneficiary of the policy is.

## § 6.7.2 Selling the Business

A buy-sell agreement may require that your spouse's interest in the business be sold to another owner or to someone else. If so, the agreement should state a method for determining the price for your spouse's interest in the business and the terms for paying the estate. Often, the price seems unreasonably low to a surviving spouse. You can discuss this issue with your attorney and decide whether or not it is advisable to have the business appraised or take other action to modify the selling price. Buy-sell agreements are often very out-of-date on the issue of reasonable price, and it is quite common for the purchasers and the family of the deceased owner to vary the price and terms for payment set out in a buy-sell agreement.

Most buy-sell agreements state that the purchase price can be paid to a deceased owner's estate over a period of years. This is usually necessary because many buyers cannot raise enough cash to pay the entire amount at once. This also may be desirable from an income tax perspective, because it may result in less total tax paid. If this is the case under an applicable buy-sell agreement, be sure you get a promissory note with reasonable interest payments due on unpaid principal and, if possible, secure the note with collateral. You must keep the original promissory note in your possession to prove the debt is owed to you if there is ever a default.

If there is no buy-sell agreement, your spouse's business partners are the most obvious purchasers of his or her interest in the business. However, when there is no buy-sell agreement, the partners may have put off discussing this unpleasant issue and may have very different ideas than you do about what should happen to your deceased spouse's interest in the business. You need expert legal and accounting help to deal with this issue.

Key employees who are not current business owners are sometimes interested in buying a business from an estate. Be prepared, however, to negotiate on price and payment terms, and do not expect that you will be paid the full purchase price in cash immediately, although this could happen. Some key employees are familiar enough with the area of business, the customers, and the suppliers that they can simply open their own competing version of the business without paying anything to the deceased owner's estate.

Be aware, however, that there are business brokers who can work with you to sell a spouse's business. They usually charge a percentage of the sale price as commission but can sometimes find a buyer for a business among competitors or others you may not be aware of. They can thus preserve at least some of the value of the business for the family.

## § 6.7.3 Closing the Business

If you come to the conclusion after serious consideration and consultation with good advisors that you are unable to operate your spouse's business (even with the help of employees) and cannot find a buyer, you may have to close the business. This should not be a snap decision, because there are many factors to consider and several avenues of advice to pursue. In general, I would advise you to do everything within reason to continue the business or sell it. Many businesses can provide significant value to the family if they continue, even if continuing them or selling them is not an easy task.

Be aware, also, that closing a business may not be as simple as it sounds. There are usually some costs and debts that must be paid. One very important consideration is whether or not the business leases space. Most commercial leases require that the rent continue to be paid even if the business vacates the premises. A common lease provision is that a business owner must personally guarantee a lease. If this is the case, the rent for any remaining lease term can become a liability of the estate. There may also be payments due to suppliers, insurance companies, employees, employee benefit plans, and contracts with customers that must be honored. If there is any unresolved litigation involving the business, the litigation will not likely terminate just because the business closes.

Even if you close a business, you should seriously consider continuing the legal existence of the business—whether it is a corporation, LLC, or partnership—for a considerable period of time so that you have a legal structure to deal with any unforeseen claims against the business that arise in the future.

## § 6.8 Litigation Involving Your Spouse or the Estate

If an estate is involved in any way in litigation, the Personal Representative represents the interest of the estate. If no Personal Representative has been appointed by a court, litigation creates a reason to do so. If your spouse was involved in any kind of litigation before death, it is very likely that the litigation will continue, with the estate being substituted for the spouse as a party to the case. Generally, litigation does not disappear when one of the parties has died.

One of the most common reasons your spouse's estate might be involved in litigation is if someone challenges the validity of the will. This is usually based on the theory that the decedent was not mentally competent to understand the meaning of the will, or that other people were wrongfully pressuring the person to create an estate plan in their favor. It is the duty of the Personal Representative to do what is possible to uphold the will, but you will need the help of an attorney who works in the area of estate administration.

Estates are also sometimes involved in litigation if there was some kind of accident involved in the death. You might want to consider a lawsuit of your own if someone else caused your spouse's death. Alternatively, someone else could sue the estate claiming that your spouse caused harm to them or a third party. Insurance could offer you protection and a legal defense, so be sure to notify any applicable insurance company (*e.g.*, homeowner's and auto) right away to preserve your rights.

One kind of litigation, however, is halted upon death: actions for legal separation and divorce are ended if either spouse dies. This means that if you or your spouse had filed for either of these actions, the case will be dismissed and you will have all of the rights of a legal spouse despite the difficulties in the marriage and the attempt to end it.

## § 6.9 Estate Assets Worksheet (Classes of Assets and How They Are Titled)

| Asset Type | Owner | Value on Date of Death |
|---|---|---|
| Real Estate | | |
| Stocks, Bonds, Mutual Funds | | |
| Bank Accounts | | |
| Life Insurance | | |
| Annuities | | |
| Retirement Plans | | |
| IRAs | | |

## § 6.10 Why the Estate Itself May Have No Assets When Your Spouse Left Significant Value

The word "estate" can have more than one meaning in the context of estate administration. The probate "estate" consists of those assets owned by the decedent in his or her name alone. The taxable "estate," in contrast, consists of all the assets in which the decedent had any form of ownership or rights. For this reason, a probate estate can have little or no value, but the taxable estate can have great value.

Joint tenancy property passes to the surviving joint tenants by operation of law, without the need for probate administration. Joint tenancy property is created by a document of ownership that shows more than one owner and states that they own the asset "as joint tenants." Those words are necessary to create a joint tenancy.

Beneficiary designation assets (such as IRAs, retirement plans, and life insurance) also pass outside the probate process by contract. An owner of any of these types of assets can designate (on a written beneficiary designation form) where they will go if he or she dies; the financial institution will be contractually bound to honor the designation and pay the value to the named beneficiary.

Trust property also usually passes outside of the probate process, because the trust document directs the trustee what to do with the trust assets after a death and gives the trustee the legal authority to transfer assets to the beneficiaries.

## § 6.11 Electing Against Your Spouse's Will

Occasionally, a circumstance arises where a surviving spouse is excluded from a deceased spouse's estate plan without having consented to this arrangement. Sometimes a decedent never created a new will after a marriage and the existing will was made before the spouses even met. Sometimes a spouse is left only a very small bequest, or a larger bequest is held in trust with someone else as trustee, and the survivor objects to this arrangement. Surviving spouses should be aware that they have what is called a "right of election" against their spouse's estate. This is essentially a lawsuit against the estate to claim a certain percentage of the estate. In Colorado, this amount is based on the length of the marriage. If the marriage lasted for at least ten years, the surviving spouse can elect to receive the maximum amount, which is one-half of the "augmented" estate. In Colorado, the augmented estate is defined by statute and includes many things. For example, it counts assets transferred to other people during the marriage under certain circumstances.

It is very common in premarital agreements to waive the right to elect against a spouse's will. If you and your spouse had a premarital agreement—which is increasingly common in second marriages—and if the agreement was made with both of the spouses being fully informed about the value of each other's estates, then you may no longer have the right of election. Even if it is viable, you should have your own attorney carefully analyze whether or not you would actually receive more from the estate by electing against the will. Sometimes you would not.

Some surviving spouses object strongly to an inheritance being held in trust and elect against the will for the purpose of getting an outright inheritance rather than periodic distributions from a trust they do not control.

## § 6.12 Closing the Estate and Distributing Assets

Before an estate can be closed, the beneficiaries must be given a complete and accurate accounting of all of the estate's receipts and disbursements. The Personal Representative should have a release signed by each of the beneficiaries in which they acknowledge in writing exactly what they are to receive from the estate before they receive it. The beneficiaries should also sign a receipt acknowledging that they received the bequest due to them.

Distribution of estate assets to beneficiaries should generally be delayed until the creditors' claims period has expired; all taxes, debts, and claims have been paid; and a closing letter has been received for the estate tax return (if there was one). There are exceptions to this rule, and sometimes partial distributions are possible before the entire administration process is complete.

The Personal Representative has the right under the probate code to make distributions in cash or in-kind. An "in-kind" distribution is a distribution of an actual asset, such as a house or shares of stock. In some cases, the nature of the assets makes it too difficult to distribute them in-kind, because the assets cannot be divided in a fair manner. A house, for example, usually cannot be distributed to several beneficiaries unless they all want to live together. In many situations, some assets are distributed in-kind and some are liquidated and distributed in cash. In others, most or all of the estate is liquidated and cash is distributed to the beneficiaries.

Aside from these considerations, the proper form of distribution is to distribute a pro rata share of all assets to all beneficiaries. For example, if 200 shares of IBM stock were distributed to two hypothetical beneficiaries, each would receive 100 shares. As noted above, this is sometimes not possible due to the nature of the assets; if this is the case, the Personal Representative should sell the asset that cannot be divided and distribute cash.

One mistake I have seen is for a Personal Representative to "cherry pick" among the most attractive assets in a way that benefits the Personal Representative or his or her favorite beneficiaries. This is a breach of fiduciary duty and must be avoided. It is also important to make distributions to all of the beneficiaries at the same time and not favor some beneficiaries with early distributions that are not made to all the beneficiaries. The beneficiaries can all agree to a distribution plan that is not pro rata and ask the Personal Representative to comply with their request, but the Personal Representative must be sure that everyone is in agreement before distributing in a manner other than a pro rata share of all assets. If you are the sole beneficiary of your spouse's estate, these issues do not apply.

When everything is completed in the administration of the estate, the Personal Representative should file a closing statement with the court to provide notice that the process is complete. The Personal Representative will retain authority to act for an additional year if any unknown issues arise. It is also possible to re-open probate in the future if an unknown asset is discovered.

# CHAPTER 7
# FILING CLAIMS FOR SURVIVOR BENEFITS

## § 7.1 Benefits Claims Process

As a surviving spouse, you may be eligible for various kinds of benefits if your spouse participated in certain programs or plans. You will need to file claims for each asset. Some assets may be provided by your spouse's employer or former employer. If so, the employer's human resources department can help you through the process. Many of these assets are also privately owned, and claims are made through the financial custodian or institution.

## § 7.2 Life Insurance

Life insurance benefits are payable to the beneficiary named by the owner of the policy on a written beneficiary designation form. In many cases, the surviving spouse is named as primary beneficiary. Sometimes other people are named as beneficiary or no one is named other than the estate of the insured.

Insurance companies typically maintain death benefit claims offices with toll-free telephone numbers to process claims. Their representatives will ask some questions when they are called to begin the claims process. They often will not give much information over the telephone, particularly if the person making the call is not the named beneficiary. They will usually send a claim form and will need a certified copy of the death certificate to be returned with the completed form. Many employers also provide life insurance as a benefit to current and retired employees, so be sure to inquire of your spouse's employer and former employers. It is common for life insurance coverage to be reduced or to end after retirement or termination of employment; but there may still be some benefits available even if your spouse was retired, so it is worth inquiring.

Life insurance companies offer different methods of paying the insurance proceeds. One very common method is to provide you with a checkbook to access the funds from an account they establish for you. You can then withdraw the funds as you need them. Many life insurance companies also provide investment and financial planning services and will offer to help you manage and invest the proceeds of the policy. If you need cash immediately for basic living expenses, then it is probably fine to just elect a lump sum distribution. If the policy is a large one and you do not need the cash immediately, you should consider deferring making the claim for a little while until your financial picture becomes more clear.

There are many options as to what to do with life insurance proceeds, and the use of a large amount of cash should be carefully considered as part of a comprehensive financial plan. It may even be beneficial to disclaim some or all of the insurance in favor of your children. A disclaimer is the legal process of saying "no thank you" to receiving an asset passing as a result of someone's death. Disclaimers are subject to a rigid process discussed in greater detail in Chapter 6. They are most often used in large estates as a method of post-mortem estate tax planning.

Because it is paid in cash and usually very quickly, life insurance is one of the most appreciated assets available to many widowed people. The beneficiary does not pay income tax on life insurance proceeds. In many cases, widowed people use some of the life insurance proceeds to purchase life insurance on their own lives as a part of their estate planning to provide a later benefit to their children. This should at least be considered as part of a comprehensive estate plan.

## § 7.3 Pension and Retirement Plans

There are two main categories of qualified tax-deferred pension and retirement plans offered by employers. "Qualified" refers to special favorable tax treatment given to these plans under the Employee Retirement Income Security Act (ERISA) and the Internal Revenue Code. The employee does not pay income tax on the money contributed to these plans during his or her working years, and the assets of the plan grow without tax until the funds are withdrawn by the employee or the employee's beneficiary. Following is a discussion of how the plans work and what your rights are to plan benefits as a surviving spouse.

## § 7.3.1 Defined Benefit Plans

Defined benefit plans are what are commonly called "pension plans." A pension plan is a form of retirement plan that pays the retiree a regular income. The plan is required to pay a certain benefit regardless of how long the employee lives or how well the stock market or economy are doing. Many pension plans offer employees the right upon retirement to designate whether the benefits will be paid only over the retired employee's lifetime and end on death or to have the payments continue after the employee's death until the death of a surviving spouse, if there is one. If the employee elects to take payments only over his or her single life, the monthly income payments will be larger than they would be if taken over two lifetimes (i.e., of the employee and spouse).

If your spouse was receiving monthly pension income, notify the pension plan administrator of the death and inquire as to what benefits are available to you as a surviving spouse. If your spouse was still working at his or her death, be sure to ask the employer's human resources director if there are pension benefits you qualify for now or in the future. It is so common for people to change jobs that you should also contact all of your spouse's former employers to make the same inquiry. Unions also sponsor or administer pension plans, so if your spouse was a member of a union, contact that union for information on pension benefits.

Pension plans are far less common than they once were. A larger proportion of employers now offer 401(k) or profit sharing plans, but there are certainly many pension plans that still exist. Private pensions are protected by ERISA and are guaranteed by the Pension Benefit Guarantee Corporation, so if you have a problem with a pension plan, your attorney will have legal support to help you collect a pension that is rightfully owed to you.

## § 7.3.2 Defined Contribution Plans

Defined contribution plans are the other major category of qualified retirement plans. The two most common kinds of defined contribution plans are profit sharing plans and 401(k) plans. The employer, employee, or both make annual contributions to these plans. The money is invested either by the plan administrator or the employee directly. Each participating employee has a separate "account" that is part of the overall plan. At an employee's retirement or death, the plan holds a certain amount of assets for him or her, depending on how much was contributed during the employee's working years. There is no guarantee that the plan will hold any particular amount of value.

It is very common for employees to move their profit sharing or 401(k) plan accounts to an IRA upon retirement or departure from an employer to work for a new employer. Like life insurance, these plan benefits pass to the beneficiary named by the employee. Unlike life insurance, surviving spouses have a legal right to receive the benefits of qualified plans governed by ERISA, which are most retirement plans of private businesses in the U.S. So if your spouse named someone else as beneficiary of a retirement plan, notify the plan administrator immediately that you want to make a claim for the benefits and you have the right to do so under ERISA. This occasionally happens if a marriage took place some time after employment commenced and the employee forgot to change the beneficiary designation form or for other reasons. Just be aware that as a surviving spouse you have a right to the plan benefits. ERISA does not apply to all retirement plans, however, and notably does not apply to plans sponsored by government agencies for their employees.

The retirement plan documents will explain what the distribution options are for 401(k) and profit sharing plans. In most cases, surviving spouse beneficiaries have the right to transfer the plan account balance into an IRA at any financial institution the spouse chooses. The transfer must be directly from the retirement plan sponsor to the new IRA custodian. If it is not, and you take personal possession of the plan assets, you will have to pay income taxes on all the funds you took.

There are two types of IRA accounts that can be opened to receive these assets, discussed below. The decision as to what kind of account to open is very important, so be sure you understand the ramifications of the choice you are making.

You can generally transfer the plan into an IRA rather than leave it with the employer plan, and you will probably want to do so to give yourself the opportunity to choose your own financial institution or advisor and your own investments. A discussion of the options for IRAs follows.

## § 7.3.3 Individual Retirement Accounts

Individual Retirement Accounts (IRAs) can be either so-called "traditional" IRAs or Roth IRAs, which have separate rules. This discussion will be primarily about traditional IRAs unless Roth IRAs are specified.

Many IRA accounts hold assets that once were part of an employer-sponsored qualified retirement plan, but which were "rolled" into an IRA at a financial institution when the employee retired or left the sponsoring employer. Other IRAs hold assets that have always been in an IRA account. The rules are the same regardless of where the assets in the IRA originated.

Like qualified plans, IRA accounts pass to the named beneficiary, rather than under a will. They are not, however, covered by ERISA, so if your spouse left an IRA to someone other than you, you do not have the clear federal legal right to the account that you have to your spouse's qualified plan accounts. Consult your attorney to analyze what rights you might have to the plan even if you are not a named beneficiary.

## § 7.3.4 Spousal Rollover IRAs

There are essentially two methods available to surviving spouses to deal with IRAs. The first method is to roll your spouse's account into your own spousal rollover IRA and withdraw it over your own life expectancy. You can take funds out of the plan without paying a penalty at any time after you reach age 59½. Remember that every penny withdrawn from an IRA or retirement plan is subject to ordinary income tax. If the owner or beneficiary withdraws funds before reaching age 59½, there generally will also be a 10 percent tax penalty on the amount withdrawn. At age 70½, you must start taking annual "required minimum distributions" (RMD) in an amount calculated on the account value and your age.

### Exceptions to the Early Withdrawal Penalty

There are a few exceptions to the 10 percent penalty imposed on withdrawal from an IRA prior to age 59½, which you might be able to use:

- If you are separated from your employment, you can take distributions without penalty if they are part of a series of substantially equal periodic payments made over your statistical life expectancy.

- Distributions taken as a result of permanent—not temporary—disability.

- Distributions taken for payment of medical expenses over 7.5 percent of your adjusted gross income.

- Distributions for payments of health insurance premiums if you have been on unemployment compensation for 12 consecutive weeks or longer.

- Distribution for expenses of higher education (not including living expenses) for yourself, your children, or your grandchildren.

- Distributions for payment for a *first-time* purchase of a home.

- Distributions for the satisfaction of a federal tax levy.

## § 7.3.5 Inherited IRAs

The second major method of receiving benefits from a spouse's IRA is to treat it as an "inherited" IRA and to take distributions based on your deceased spouse's statistical life expectancy rather than your own. This option is most often used by people who are widowed before they reach 59½, who need funds from their spouse's IRA as soon as possible, and are younger than their deceased spouse. If they roll the IRA into a spousal IRA and take distributions before they turn 59½, they will have to pay a 10 percent penalty. If their spouse was older than they are, they may have penalty-free access to an inherited IRA earlier than would be possible from a spousal rollover IRA. If your spouse was younger than you, an inherited IRA will mean that you will be older than 59½ when you have penalty-free access to the account.

If you decide to take your spouse's IRA as an inherited IRA rather than a spousal rollover, you may need to begin taking RMDs each year. If your spouse was over 70½ at death, an RMD must be taken for the year of death based upon the decedent's life expectancy under the Uniform Lifetime Table (an IRS life expectancy table). Thereafter, the RMDs are calculated each year using the longer of your life expectancy using the Single Life Table (an IRS life-expectancy table) or the life expectancy of your deceased spouse under the Single Life Table.

If your spouse was below age 70½ at death, you can defer the RMDs until the year when your spouse would have reached 70½. Thereafter, the RMDs are based on your life expectancy under the Single Life Table. The most common reason that widowed people choose to take IRAs as inherited rather than spousal rollovers is to gain earlier access to the funds. This is obviously an individual decision that should be thoroughly analyzed and discussed with a knowledgeable accountant and/or attorney to weigh the advantages and disadvantages of the various options in each case. You will need someone, preferably a knowledgeable accountant, to help you calculate the RMDs each year when you are required to take them, either after you turn 70½ or after your spouse would have turned 70½, depending on the method you choose.

In rolling over a qualified plan or your spouse's IRA, you must first be clear in your own mind as to which kind of IRA you are choosing, spousal rollover or inherited. You must also be certain to give specific instructions (in writing) to the new IRA custodian as to which kind of account you are opening. The funds from your spouse's IRA or qualified plan must be transferred directly to the new IRA account and *not* paid to you personally. They must be received by the new account no later than 60 days after they are removed from the decedent's account. If you receive the funds personally and they are not in a rollover or inherited account 60 days after withdrawal from your spouse's account, you will be subject to income tax on the entire amount (plus penalties if you are under 59½). I have seen this happen inadvertently with inexperienced employees at financial institutions when dealing with clients who do not understand the complex rules governing IRAs.

The decisions about how to take retirement plan and IRA distributions are somewhat complex and require careful analysis. These assets are often a significant part of a widowed person's financial security.

### Time Limits

If your spouse was at least 70½ at death and required to take RMDs, you must start taking RMDs by no later than December 31 of the year following your spouse's death or face a possible penalty of 50 percent of what should have been distributed. If you are younger than your spouse, you can avoid this problem by rolling the account into a spousal rollover before that date and taking the benefits based on your own life expectancy.

### § 7.3.6 Roth IRAs

Roth IRAs are very different from traditional IRAs. The funds contributed to Roth IRAs are not tax-deferred and there are no minimum distribution rules during an owner's lifetime. After the owner's death, however, the same rules apply to Roth IRAs as traditional IRAs. A surviving spouse can roll a Roth IRA into his or her own spousal rollover Roth IRA. The spouse will then be subject to the 10 percent penalty for withdrawing funds from the Roth IRA prior to turning 59½. If you choose not to roll the Roth IRA into your own spousal rollover IRA, you will be subject to the same rules as for traditional inherited IRAs.

### § 7.3.7 Complexity

The rules governing retirement plan and IRA assets are complex, although Congress has simplified them somewhat in the last few years. The penalty for making mistakes is usually current taxation that could have been avoided or tax penalties of 10 percent to 50 percent. Get the advice you need to be sure you understand what you are doing with these assets and that you have complete information on the options available.

## § 7.4 Veterans Benefits

If your spouse was a military veteran, you may be eligible for certain benefits. To get information and to make claims, you will need an official copy of your spouse's Veteran's DD-214, which is the official discharge form for military service. If you cannot find this document for your spouse, you can request one from the National Personnel Records Center by submitting the appropriate request form. You will also need the following:

1. State certified death certificate;

2. Certified copy of your marriage license;

3. Certified copies of each child's birth certificate (if applying for any children's benefits);

4. Social Security numbers for you and your spouse; and

5. Name and address of the Personal Representative of your spouse's estate (if one has been appointed).

Veterans are usually eligible for burial in a national cemetery, payments towards burial expenses, a headstone or marker, and an American flag to drape over the coffin. The Department of Veterans Affairs may pay for transportation of the deceased to the national cemetery nearest the deceased's last residence. There is no charge for burial of a veteran in a national cemetery. If you would prefer that your spouse be buried in a private cemetery, you can still apply for reimbursement of some of the costs.

There are other benefits available in some cases, including educational benefits for children, dependency and indemnity compensation (DIC), and medical care for some spouses and children. Many veterans maintained service-related life insurance. The Department of Veterans Affairs has a website at www.va.gov/.

The Denver Regional Office for the Department of Veterans Affairs is located at 155 Van Gordon Street, Lakewood, Colorado 80228 and can be reached at 303-985-0618 or 800-827-1000.

# CHAPTER 8
# SOCIAL SECURITY, MEDICARE, MEDICAID, AND HEALTH INSURANCE

—————————

## § 8.1 Social Security

Social Security is a federal program that provides benefits to many—but not all—surviving spouses and some dependent children under several different programs. Entitlement to Social Security benefits is earned through work and payment of Social Security taxes. As a surviving spouse, you may be eligible for benefits as a result of your spouse's work history and you will retain your own eligibility based on your work history. A surviving spouse, however, may be eligible for benefits even if he or she has never contributed to Social Security. The number of years a person needs to have worked in order for survivors to be eligible for benefits depends on the age of the decedent at death. The younger a person was at death, the fewer years he or she needed to have worked in order to provide survivors benefits.

Another factor in the Social Security equation is the concept of "full retirement age." For people born before 1938, full retirement age is 65 years. For people born later, the age is greater than 65 years, by months or years. It gradually increases and is now age 67 for people born in 1960 or later. Social Security can advise you as to your own full retirement age, and this is an important factor for some younger widows and widowers in deciding when to begin receiving survivors benefits if they have the resources to choose to delay it.

Some workers are not eligible for Social Security because they are insured under the Railroad Retirement Act instead. Some people are granted an exemption from contributing to Social Security as a member of a religious group that opposes the Social Security system. If your spouse was granted this exemption, you may not be eligible for survivors benefits.

Several groups of surviving family members may be eligible for benefits, including the following:

- Surviving spouses of either gender are eligible for full benefits at age 65 or older (for widowed persons born before 1940) or reduced benefits as early as age 60 (or age 50 if the widowed person is disabled under the Social Security definition of disability), so-called "widow(er)s rights."

- Surviving spouses of either gender of any age if they are caring for at least one child of the decedent who is eligible for child's benefits and is age 16 or younger or who is disabled, so-called "father's or mother's" benefits.

- Unmarried children under 18 (or up to 19 if they are attending elementary or secondary school) can receive benefits, "child's benefits." Children of a decedent of any age who are disabled and became disabled before age 22 are also eligible.

- Dependent parents of a decedent who are at least 62 and for whom the decedent was providing at least half of their support are also eligible.

- There is also a one-time, lump-sum death benefit of $255 that can be made only to surviving spouses and minor children under certain circumstances. There are certain work history requirements for eligibility for this benefit.

## § 8.2 How to Apply for Social Security Benefits

You should promptly apply for Social Security survivors benefits because some programs start payment from the date of application rather than the date of death. You can apply by telephone (800-772-1213 from 7:00 a.m. to 7:00 p.m. Monday through Friday) or at any Social Security office. Even if you want or need to apply in person, start with a phone call so you can make an appointment and familiarize yourself with the information you will need to provide.

You will need to provide the following documentation:

1. State certified death certificate for your spouse.

2. Your deceased spouse's Social Security number (this appears on Colorado death certificates).

3. Your own Social Security number.

4. A state certified copy of your own birth certificate.

5. A state certified copy of your marriage certificate.

6. Dependent children's Social Security numbers, if any.

7. Your spouse's most recent year's W-2 form or federal self-employment tax return (these will be attached to the most recent income tax return he or she filed).

8. Name and account number of a bank account where you want your benefits to be direct deposited.

If you were already receiving benefits as a wife or husband of a retired worker during your spouse's lifetime, Social Security will convert your payments to widow(er)s payments. If you are receiving benefits based on your own work history, Social Security will determine if you could receive more in widow(er)'s benefits and will and pay you whichever amount is higher. You cannot receive both kinds of benefits.

The amount paid to you as a widow(er) is based on your deceased spouse's work history of earnings and taxes paid. A formula is applied based on the survivors' ages and relationship to the decedent. A surviving spouse of full retirement age or older receives 100 percent of the decedent's basic benefit. A surviving spouse age 60 or older, but less than full retirement age, receives 71 to 99 percent of the decedent's basic benefit. The reduced payments remain reduced permanently; in other words, they do not increase after the spouse reaches full retirement age. For this reason, some surviving spouses decline to accept survivors benefits until they reach full retirement age themselves. A widowed person of any age with a child under age 16 receives 75 percent of the decedent's basic benefit. Children receive 75 percent of the decedent's basic benefit. There is a maximum amount the family group can receive, generally between 150 percent and 180 percent of the decedent's basic benefit.

If you continue to work while receiving survivors benefits and you are younger than full retirement age, your benefits may be reduced if your earnings exceed certain limits. The amount of the limits generally changes annually. You should contact Social Security to get specific information on this figure each year since this information will be important to your decision about continuing your own employment. Once you reach full retirement age, your own earnings will not affect your benefits. If you work and your benefits are reduced, this will not reduce benefits to children or dependent parents.

If you remarry prior to age 60, you will lose your survivor benefits. Remarriage after age 60 will not prevent you from getting benefits based on your former spouse's work history. There is a common misconception that remarriage permanently deprives a widowed person of eligibility for Social Security benefits based on a deceased spouse's work record; based on this misconception, numbers of older Americans choose to live with a new companion rather than marry that person despite moral or religious misgivings. Remarriage after widowhood should be considered carefully for many reasons, but if you are at least 60 years old, loss of Social Security is not one of them. In addition, if the new marriage ends in divorce, you can apply to reinstate your benefits as a surviving spouse of your prior marriage.

Sometimes it is unclear as to who qualifies as a "widow(er)" for Social Security purposes. As noted elsewhere, Colorado recognizes common law marriage, but survivors without a marriage license, regardless of how long they lived together, can face difficulties in qualifying for survivors benefits in many contexts. If this applies to you, be aware that Social Security will consider you to be a widow(er) if you meet any one of the following conditions:

1. You were married to the decedent for at least the nine months prior to his or her death (with a few exceptions such as accidental death or death in the line of duty in the armed services);

2. You are the biological parent of the decedent's child (this will apply to you even if the child is no longer living);

3. You *legally adopted* at least one child of the decedent before the child reached age 18;

4. The decedent *legally adopted* one of your children during your marriage before the child reached age 18;

5. If you were ceremonially married to the decedent, but later discovered that the marriage was invalid (usually because the decedent had previously been married to someone else and not validly divorced from that person), you may still be eligible for widow(er) benefits provided that:

a. You married the decedent in good faith, not knowing of any imped-
iment to the marriage;

b. You were living with the decedent at the time of his or her death;

c. For periods prior to 1991, there is no one else entitled to widow(er)'s
benefits who still has status as a legal widow(er); and

d. The invalid marriage resulted from a prior marriage or divorce or a
legal defect in your marriage to the decedent.

Obviously, it is easier to prove a marriage by producing a marriage license,
and evidentiary questions can arise or be more complicated if you don't have
one. But pursuing a claim for survivors benefits for yourself and your minor
children can be well worth the effort. If necessary, you should consult an
attorney who practices in the area of Social Security law to help you.

## § 8.3 When Do Social Security Benefits End?

Social Security widow(er)'s benefits end upon the following events:

1. Your death;

2. You become entitled to your own Social Security retirement benefit,
which is greater than the widow(er)s benefit you had been receiving
(you do not get your own benefit plus a widow(er)s benefit, only the
greater of the two);

3. Your disability ends, if you were receiving widow(er)s benefits based on
your own disability;

4. You remarry before reaching age 60 and are not disabled.

Social Security mother's or father's insurance ends on the following events:

1. There are no children of the decedent under the age of 16 or disabled;

2. You become eligible for widow(er)s benefits (you do not get both); or

3. You remarry.

Social Security child's benefits end on the following events:

1. The child reaches 18 (or 19 if enrolled in elementary or secondary
school); or

2. The child marries.

This information is not intended to be a complete summary of Social Security law or to deal with individual situations, but is meant to serve as an introductory guide and to cover the most common situations. In general, you should start with contacting Social Security by phone (and in person, if necessary). If you believe that you are wrongfully being denied benefits, you can then consult an attorney who has expertise in Social Security matters.

In our law practice, the most common problems arise for people who are disabled. Some conditions are accepted as conclusive of disability by Social Security, but many are not. We also often encounter younger widows who do not have children under 16 who are unpleasantly surprised to find that they have no widows benefits until they are 60. Men are still sometimes surprised to find that they do qualify for widowers benefits or benefits as the parent of a child under 16 or a disabled child.

## § 8.4 Medicare and Medicaid

People are often confused by the similarity of the names of these two government programs. They are fundamentally different, however. Medicare is a federal program that provides medical and hospital insurance to persons age 65 and older. Eligibility is based on an individual's work history or the work history of a spouse or deceased spouse. Some disabled people younger than 65 may also be eligible for Medicare. Income and asset ownership are irrelevant in qualifying for Medicare.

Medicare *does not* pay for long-term care. It will pay for 20 days per year of skilled nursing care requiring the services of a registered nurse. Individuals eligible for Medicare must pay premiums for both the medical and hospital benefits. If premiums are not paid, coverage will be denied.

Medicaid, however, is a joint state and federal program that requires needs-based qualification due to low income and very few assets. Generally, in Colorado, people under age 65 become eligible for Medicaid only if they are also eligible for other needs-based welfare programs. Many people over age 65 also eventually become eligible for Medicaid payment of their nursing home costs. They may be eligible for both Medicare and Medicaid at the same time. For eligible people under age 65 who are too young for Medicare, Medicaid can provide payment for medical treatment from physicians and hospitals.

Congress has made it more difficult over time to become eligible for Medicaid payment of nursing home costs unless the applicant is essentially impoverished. At one time, it was possible for people to give away assets to other family members and to become eligible for Medicaid payment of nursing home costs soon thereafter in order to preserve family wealth for other family members. That is no longer the case. Many people have heard stories about other people who have managed to accomplish this and have the misconception that giving assets to a spouse or adult children will result in immediate eligibility for Medicaid. Now, if assets are transferred to a spouse, they are still counted as the applicant's property. If they are given to other people (like adult children), the transfer will result in ineligibility for a period of time based on the value of the assets divided by the average monthly cost of nursing home care in the state if an application for Medicaid is made within 36 months of the transfer. There are different rules for married couples if one spouse remains outside of a nursing home.

There are some exceptions, but for widowed people over age 65, Medicaid will pay for nursing home care only in very specific instances and after an application that requests exhaustive financial records. A single applicant can only retain very limited assets and must have monthly income below a level set each year in order to qualify.

I have never heard anyone say that they want to live in a nursing home. Despite the almost universal reluctance to spend time in one, close to half of the population now spends at least some time during their lives in a nursing home. Sometimes this is only for a short period, to recuperate from surgery or an illness, or, sadly, to die after being forced to leave a hospital after insurance will no longer pay for inpatient care. Statistically, most nursing home residents spend less than three years in a facility. In a small percentage of cases, however, people may live in a nursing home for more than three years. In many facilities, regardless of how long a patient stays, a majority of nursing home residents spend all of their assets on their care and then qualify for Medicaid. The result is that there is nothing for the family members to inherit.

I am often asked about ways to preserve a person's assets for the family while qualifying the person for Medicaid payment of nursing home care. This question is usually asked after the person has been diagnosed with some form of dementia or other condition that will eventually require daily care. While none of us wants to be in the position of needing long-term care, it happens to many of us despite our wishes to the contrary.

The harsh reality is that there are only three ways of paying for nursing home care. One is to pay for it personally (and possibly use all of your assets in the process). The second way is to become impoverished and apply and qualify for Medicaid. The third source of payment is long-term care insurance.

Long-term care insurance is regulated by state law. It can pay for in-home care and/or nursing home care. In-home care is more expensive. As of this writing, in-home care in the Denver metro area costs around $25.00 per hour, or around $4,000 per month, depending on whether or not family members can spend some time during each week caring for the person.

There are some reputable services that provide in-home caregivers, but they are not cheap. Families sometimes hire caregivers they find through newspaper want ads. While this may work out well, I have seen several situations where caregivers hired in this way without references, licensing, or bonding have victimized the ill person. They may steal money or property from the person, talk them into signing a power of attorney that gives the caregiver access to bank accounts, and even have the person sign over deeds to real estate. People needing long-term care are often vulnerable to coercion or exploitation. I would not recommend this method of getting help for anyone needing long-term care.

The difficulty in finding and paying for good, honest, competent, dependable, and compassionate home caregivers at a reasonable cost often results in a nursing home becoming absolutely necessary despite the person's wish to stay at home. Medicaid does not pay enough to cover the cost of 24-hour, seven-days-a-week care at home. Medicaid also does not find caregivers. I have seen situations where the only caregivers the family has been able to find and pay have been criminals, drug addicts, and people who victimize and abuse the elderly and ill.

## § 8.5 Long-Term Care

Long-term care insurance policies have different design features, but they usually provide for a certain dollar amount per month towards in-home care, and that amount will not pay for the typical actual cost of this kind of care. Nursing home care can be less expensive and the coverage may be for a greater percentage of the cost. The greater the benefits provided by the policy, the more expensive the premiums will be. Some people compromise by deciding that long-term care insurance will be only a supplement for them and that they will pay for at least part of the cost of their care rather than trying to buy insurance to cover all of the cost. It is also possible to reduce the cost by agreeing to an eligibility waiting period, which will require the individual to pay for the first number of months of care personally and then have any longer period paid for by insurance.

There are a number of insurance companies that sell long-term care insurance in Colorado. I would advise comparing at least three different companies when considering this insurance. You should have a very thorough conversation with any broker selling this kind of insurance about all the details of the policies. Some of the features you should ask about are inflation protection, eligibility waiting periods, premium increases, and the ability to stop paying premiums if you are actually receiving policy benefits. Whenever you buy insurance, ask for the rating of the insurance company. If the company goes out of business due to financial failure, you will have paid your premiums for nothing. Unfortunately, the first time that many people think about long-term care insurance is when they or a family member is diagnosed with a serious health problem. It will then be impossible to qualify for a policy.

While none of us like to think about the possibility that we will need long-term care, there are many good arguments that of the three methods of payment, if ever needed, long-term care insurance can be the least expensive, most flexible, and easiest to manage. Regardless of how you feel about long-term care insurance, all widowed people should give the topic of how to pay for long-term care, if ever necessary, serious thought as early in life as possible. The answer for some people will be to accept that all of their money may someday need to be spent on their care, that they may then need to apply for Medicaid, and that they may not have enough assets to pass anything to their children after their death. If this is acceptable to you, then you have made your decision and you have every right to make this choice. If you have limited assets and income, this may be the only practical choice. If you would prefer to preserve some of your assets for your children or grandchildren, then long-term care insurance may be the easiest and cheapest way to accomplish this goal. Alternatively, some financial advisors suggest that the children purchase and own a life insurance policy on a parent's life in order to secure some kind of inheritance for themselves in a manner that will not impact the parent.

Regardless of your choice in this matter, you should have a frank conversation with your adult children to let them know your desires. Some adult children may offer to pay long-term care insurance premiums for you if you cannot afford them or simply don't want to pay them. It is always easier to deal with these issues long before there is a need and certainly before there is a serious medical problem.

## § 8.6 Qualifying for Medicaid

There are attorneys in Colorado who focus a great deal of their practice on qualifying people for Medicaid while preserving assets for the family. They often identify themselves as "elder law" practitioners; if you are interested in this topic, you can locate attorneys through local and state bar associations who can discuss it knowledgeably with you.

One strategy that some people use can be very risky: giving assets to adult children (usually) so as to impoverish oneself and thereby become eligible for Medicaid in the future. Parents sometimes do this, usually at the request of adult children, with the expectation that the children would give the assets back to the parent if requested or at least made available for the parent's benefit. Sometimes this works out well, but other times it does not. There have been cases where the parent has later requested the return of money or property only to find that it has been spent, or divided by the court in a child's divorce, or attached by a child's creditors, or levied by the IRS for a child's unpaid taxes.

I would caution anyone considering this course of action to consult an attorney who practices in the area of Medicaid planning and a trusted accountant. No one should ever rush into a decision on this issue. Parents should never be made to feel guilty about wanting to retain their own assets to pay for their own care, even if this means their children will not inherit much from them. While other attorneys may have differing opinions, I believe this course of action to be very dangerous and filled with the potential for bad results. Despite this caution, there may be situations where this course of action works out well; but usually there needs to be some significant assets involved, some considerable time to plan, and a knowledgeable and ethical attorney involved.

## § 8.7 Medicare and Supplemental Health Insurance

For people over 65, Medicare pays for most—but not all—medical and hospital costs. Many people therefore buy so-called Medicare supplement of "medigap" insurance to pay the portion of medical expenses that Medicare expects individuals to pay. Several major health insurance companies offer these policies. This kind of insurance is regulated by state government. It has deductibles and other options within the regulatory framework. If you need expensive medication, be sure to inquire about prescription drug coverage. Congress passed a Medicare drug benefit law in 2004, but it likely will not cover all prescription costs for all people.

## § 8.8 Private Individual Health Insurance

If you are widowed before you reach age 65, you will generally not be eligible for Medicare unless you are disabled and have gone through a Social Security disability determination process. With the current cost of medical care, an accident or any unforeseen health problem could devastate you financially. If you have dependent children, their need is as great as yours.

Health insurance coverage is an important social and political issue that affects all groups of people, but coverage for widowed persons who are not yet 65 and who are not in the workforce is a neglected but vitally important issue. If you were covered by a spouse's policy, you will eventually need to obtain your own coverage. If you are working, you may be able to obtain health insurance through your employment even if you didn't enroll in the plan while you were married because you were covered by your spouse's plan. If your employer will pay for your coverage, then you are lucky indeed.

Many employers who offer health insurance do not pay for it, but do offer it through a "cafeteria plan" that at least makes the premiums payable with pre-tax dollars and therefore less expensive for you. If you are interviewing for a job, be sure to ask about health insurance eligibility, if there is a plan offered, and whether or not there is a waiting period for new employees to be covered.

Employers do not have to offer health insurance at all. Even if they do, they do not have to cover employees who work less than full-time as defined by the employer plan. "Full-time" is frequently defined as 35 hours per week of work in employer plans, although other hourly requirements are possible. In many cases, it will be necessary to move from part-time employment to full-time employment simply to qualify for health insurance. Some widowed persons realize that they need to return to work for the primary reason of obtaining health insurance.

Another source for health insurance is individual private coverage available directly through a health insurance company or through a broker who finds this kind of coverage for individuals. Many insurance companies sell their policies over the Internet. A company may or may not be a good choice for you. Colorado has an Insurance Commission that can give you information about complaints made against insurance companies or brokers; see the Division of Insurance website at www.dora.state.co.us/insurance/.

Unlike employer-provided policies, which legally must provide coverage to everyone eligible for the employer's plan regardless of health history, private health insurance companies can reject an applicant or can exclude certain pre-existing conditions. If you have a history of health problems, you may have difficulty getting private coverage. In the past, some individuals have omitted certain health information from applications for private insurance in order to get coverage. Do not be tempted to do this. If you do, in the event you need to make a claim for payment for care for any reason, the insurance company can deny payment on the grounds that the policy was obtained fraudulently. The company can do this even if the current need has nothing to do with the concealed prior condition. It is often frustrating to go through this process and be rejected for a prior health problem that does not seem very serious or that has been resolved. Health insurance companies look at the applicant's mental health problems and treatment as well as strictly physical problems. If you are not making progress getting coverage, you might be well served by working with a reputable health insurance broker.

Other sources of health insurance are voluntary organizations, such as AARP and some religious, alumni, or other organizations. In my experience, their policies are not as desirable as employer plans or private policies because the applicant has fewer options about plan features and the coverage simply is not as extensive.

When evaluating health insurance policies, the premium cost is obviously the first consideration, although you will usually have some options that can affect the premiums. It is very important to get clear information about deductibles, co-payment amounts, the doctors and hospitals you can use (and have the policy make the payments), the percentage of costs the policy will pay and the percentage you will be responsible for, what prescription coverage the policy provides, and any excluded conditions. Some people want a great deal of choice as to doctors and hospitals, but this flexibility usually adds to the cost of a policy. HMO plans and Kaiser Permanente have smaller lists of doctors and hospitals, and you generally must use them in order to have the plan pay the cost, but their premiums are generally lower. Some people do not take much prescription medication and are willing to forego extensive coverage in this area. I would caution everyone, though, to realize that your health can change in the future in unforeseeable ways and that anyone, regardless of health—and through no fault of their own—can be an accident victim and suffer injuries that require costly care and medication.

I cannot overemphasize the seriousness of the need for you to be covered by health insurance at all times, and the need for you to deal with this issue as quickly as possible and to give it your highest priority of attention. Health insurance coverage is one major exception to the general rule that almost no financial decisions need to be made in a hurry.

## § 8.9 CoverColorado

CoverColorado is a Colorado state program that offers individual health insurance for people who have applied for, but were denied, private individual coverage. Some pre-existing conditions make it easy to qualify for this program. To get this coverage, you must apply for it, and you must have evidence that you have been denied private coverage. CoverColorado has many of the same features as other health insurance, including annual deductibles. This insurance is not free and the cost can be quite high for low-deductible policies. This program is, however, another resource to pursue if individual or employer coverage is not available to you.

## § 8.10 COBRA and Your Spouse's Employer Group Health Insurance

If you and your spouse were covered under your spouse's employer's group health insurance plan, a federal law known as COBRA requires the employer to offer you continuing coverage for 18 months after your spouse's death. The employer must give you written notice of this right, but if you don't hear anything about it within a fairly short time, you should call the employer's human resources department and ask about this issue.

While you must be offered coverage, the employer does not have to pay for any part of your insurance; you must pay the entire amount of the premiums yourself. The cost may shock you, but the risk of having to pay for treatment for a serious health problem or accident is so great that it is worth paying for the premiums, at least until you can secure other coverage.

The COBRA notice will give you a date by which you must accept this coverage. It is vitally important for you to respond in writing within the time limit. If you accept the coverage, you can cancel it at any time during the 18-month coverage period. After 18 months, the employer is no longer required to offer you COBRA coverage unless you have suffered certain serious disabilities during the 18-month period, in which case the coverage may be extended for a longer period. Some larger employers provide more extensive coverage voluntarily or through collective bargaining agreements.

You should obtain complete written information on your rights to health insurance through your spouse's employment as soon as possible. Unless you are positive that you have coverage immediately available to you through your own employment, it is usually a good idea to accept the COBRA coverage, despite its cost, until you can calmly analyze what health insurance is available to you and compare the features and costs of COBRA and other insurance. Remember, though, that COBRA is a short-term solution to the health insurance issue and that you should proceed to get your own coverage either through your own employment or a private policy as soon as possible.

# § 8.11 Disability Insurance: Who Needs It, How It Is Taxed

Disability insurance replaces the income of workers who are disabled during their working years. If you are working and know that you need to rely on your own employment to support yourself after your spouse's death, you should investigate disability income insurance. Disability is more common than many people realize—and if you no longer have your spouse's salary, you need to plan for this contingency. Your expenses won't go away if you can no longer work and they are likely to increase if you have a health problem.

Many employers provide disability income insurance, and if your employer does, it is likely to be the least expensive option for you. If your employer does not offer this kind of insurance, you will need to contact a broker who deals with these policies. Due to a large number of claims made in the recent past, private disability coverage is far more expensive and difficult to obtain than it once was.

There are some important features of disability policies that you should understand. The threshold issue is how the policy defines "disability." Many policies will not make payments to you unless you can prove that you are completely disabled and unable to do any kind of work whatsoever. This is obviously very difficult to prove. Insurance companies have denied payment to people in lucrative professions on the grounds that, for example, while they can no longer be an accountant, they could be a janitor (or other arguments along this vein). Other policies, which I think are more desirable, define disability as being unable to perform the duties of your profession or job at the time the claim is made.

Another important issue is who pays for the premiums. If the employer pays the premiums, any benefits you receive from the policy will be subject to income tax. If you pay the premiums, the benefits will be tax-free. The income you get from the coverage will therefore be significantly greater. Your employer will permit you to pay the premiums yourself for an employer-sponsored plan. You will be paying your own premiums for an individual policy.

Disability insurance can be difficult to get unless it is offered through an employer, and it can be quite expensive. The younger you are and the fewer assets you have dictate how important having this coverage is. If you have significant assets and could support yourself and your dependents for the rest of your reasonable life expectancy, then disability insurance is not likely to be very important for you, particularly if you are already near retirement age. For a younger person with few assets, though, the inability to work could be devastating financially.

# CHAPTER 9
# MONEY, BUDGET, AND CREDIT

## § 9.1 Immediate Sources of Cash

Many widowed people fear that all of their deceased spouse's funds will be "frozen" and unavailable for the family's support for a considerable period of time. In most cases, some funds become available very quickly. Often, a large part of the estate may not be distributable for many months. In other cases, particularly if the surviving spouse is the sole beneficiary of the estate and there are not significant debts, most of the estate can be distributed within a few months. Each case depends on factors specific to that situation.

Many people become frustrated by the length of time it can take to gain access to all of an estate's assets. But in some circumstances, legal and debt issues simply must be resolved prior to distribution to protect the Personal Representative and the beneficiaries from personal liability. Despite these issues, there are some readily available sources of funds available to surviving spouses, which may apply to your situation.

If you and your spouse had bank accounts or money market accounts at a brokerage in joint tenancy, you have the right to all of the funds in the accounts immediately. If you and your spouse had certificates of deposit, federal banking law provides that a surviving spouse can withdraw those funds before the maturity date without an early withdrawal penalty after the death of a spouse.

If there is a probate estate, your attorney can help you apply for a family allowance and exempt property allowance from the estate assets. The total for both of these allowances is $50,000 as of the date of this book. These allowances can be distributed to you before other bills are paid and before any actual bequests are distributed. They do not reduce the amount of your remaining inheritance if your spouse's estate is divided into shares for you and other beneficiaries.

Remember that probate can be opened in Colorado five days after a death. If you are in urgent need of funds and need access to money held in the name of your deceased spouse, be sure to tell your attorney of this need so that he or she can expedite the probate process and make these claims for you.

If you and your spouse owned investments in a joint tenancy brokerage account, you have the right to sell some or all of those assets to obtain cash. You can also borrow against the account. This is called "margining" the account and is somewhat risky. People sometimes borrow against investment accounts when they need cash and the market is not doing very well, in hopes that the value of their investments will go up in the future and they can sell assets later and pay back the loan at a time when the market is better. The risk is that if the value of the entire account were to go below the loan amount, you would be liable for repaying the entire amount immediately in cash. This can happen if the stock market is going down for a continuous period, as it sometimes does. Many people consider margining an account to be unreasonably risky, but it is available to owners of investment accounts.

If your spouse had life insurance and you are the named beneficiary, you will probably be able to collect the policy benefits very quickly once you obtain a death certificate and the insurance company claim form. Many employers offer life insurance to their employees, and the spouse may not be aware of its existence. Some health insurance plans also include a life insurance benefit. Be sure to inquire about these possibilities with your spouse's employer.

If your spouse participated in a qualified retirement plan through an employer, then you have the right to plan benefits, which often become available quickly. Contact your spouse's employer's human resources department for information on how to claim plan benefits. If your spouse had IRAs or annuities, it is likely that you are the account beneficiary. If so, funds from these accounts can become available to you very quickly. These assets are often held at banks, investment brokerages, and insurance companies.

Many creditors will work with families after a death if they are given notice that there has been a death, that you are working on collecting assets, and that you will pay debts as soon as it is feasible. There is a more extensive discussion about debts and creditors' claims in Chapter 6.

## § 9.2 Determining Your Income and Expenses From Now On

Your own individual income should not be affected by your spouse's death, provided that you continue to work if you were working before the death and if you continue to treat any investments you own individually just as you did before the death.

Your spouse's income from employment will stop, but other sources of income may continue and some new sources of income might become available to you. The first step is to collect your spouse's bank records and go through them carefully to analyze his or her sources of income. While wages and salary will stop, be aware that if your spouse worked on a commission basis, some commissions may still be owed to his or her estate for transactions that close after the date of death.

If your spouse was collecting Social Security, you may be able to collect his or her benefits too, although the amount will be different. See Chapter 8 for a more detailed discussion of rights to Social Security.

If your spouse was collecting a pension from an employer plan, it is very likely that there will be a survivor's benefit for you. A pension plan is a type of retirement plan that pays a monthly amount to retirees. Some pension plans give employees a choice of taking their plan benefits over the joint lives of the employee and the employee's surviving spouse (which will result in a lower monthly payment) or taking the benefit over the employee's life only, with benefits terminating at death. The latter usually results in a higher monthly benefit. If your spouse chose the single-life option, the pension payments will stop when he or she dies.

Some pension plans also permit employees to designate other people (such as children) to receive a reduced benefit after the employee's death. Sometimes a beneficiary designation names other beneficiaries for plan benefits because it was signed prior to a marriage and never updated.

The Employee Retirement Income Security Act (ERISA) is a federal law that governs many (but not all) pension plans. ERISA gives surviving spouses of participants in ERISA plans the legal rights to the plan benefits even if someone else was named as the beneficiary. If you are in this situation, you should immediately notify the administrator of the pension plan in writing that you are the surviving spouse and that you are making a claim for plan benefits. Enclose a copy of your marriage certificate and also notify your attorney of this issue.

If your spouse was a participant in a profit sharing plan, 401(k) plan, 403(b) plan, or other retirement plan and was still working at his or her death, you should be able to claim the plan benefits. Most widowed people in this situation take the plan benefits and roll them into an IRA. Depending on the ages of the employee and the surviving spouse, the IRA can become a source of monthly income. See Chapter 7 for a more detailed discussion of how to take IRA benefits.

If your spouse owned an annuity through an insurance company and you are the named beneficiary, then you might be able to begin to receive regular income from the annuity. Retirement plan benefits and annuity payments are classified as ordinary income for income tax purposes.

If your spouse owned stocks and bonds that produce interest and dividends, those dividends and income will continue to be produced if the assets are retained in the form they were in during your spouse's lifetime. Stock dividends are taxed as ordinary income. Interest from bonds may be taxable as ordinary income or may be tax-exempt for federal or both federal and state income tax purposes, depending on their tax characteristics. If you inherit these investments, they will continue to produce income.

If your spouse was receiving income from someone who owed him or her money under a promissory note, that obligation should continue and the note payments should be available to you if you inherit the note.

If your spouse owned any kind of rental property, the lease obligations will continue and you will receive the rental income if you inherit the rental property.

If your spouse owned a business, his or her business partners might have a contractual obligation to buy out your spouse's interest in the business and either pay for the business in a lump sum or make periodic payments until the amount is paid off. If you inherit the business, the payments will be made to you. There is more detailed discussion of business ownership in Chapter 6 and Chapter 15.

You will be able to gather information on income sources from bank books and computerized records (such as Quicken) if your spouse kept them. Review your income tax returns for the last several years; they can give you information about sources of income you might not be aware of as well as letting you know what your tax liability has been and might be in the future. You will also receive information from incoming mail as time passes. Keep an accurate and complete list of all income items you discover.

## § 9.3 Determining Your Expenses and Setting Up a Realistic Budget

Get a paper ledger book or set up a computer spreadsheet to help you track expenses. Begin by using bank ledgers and check and credit card copies to make a complete month-by-month list of what you and your spouse spent money on during the last two years of your life together, beginning with the most recent year and working backwards. Be as complete as possible. Many people underestimate how much money they spend each month and forget to include seasonal or occasional categories such as travel.

The purpose of this exercise is to determine how much money you will need each year to maintain your current lifestyle. Other decisions also flow from this information, such as whether or not to move, sell assets, get a job (if you haven't been working), or change careers. Some expenses will stay the same now that you are widowed, such as your current housing costs. Some expenses will go down, such as groceries. Others may actually increase, e.g., if you were covered under your spouse's employer's health insurance plan and you now must pay for a more expensive individual policy. Or, if your spouse's employer offered dental or vision coverage, you may now have to pay for those expenses yourself. If your spouse had expensive hobbies or leisure activities, these expense items will go away. If your spouse was ill for an extended period of time and had significant out-of-pocket expenses for medication or other items, those expenses will be gone. You can use the following chart as a sample template.

| Expenses for (Month) (Year) | | | | | |
|---|---|---|---|---|---|
| Expense Categories | Expenditures | | | | |
| **Food** | | | | | |
| Groceries | | | | | |
| Restaurants | | | | | |
| **Housing** | | | | | |
| Mortgage/Rent | | | | | |
| Water | | | | | |
| Heat/Lights | | | | | |
| Phone | | | | | |
| Cell Phone | | | | | |
| Maintenance/Repairs | | | | | |
| Cleaning Services | | | | | |
| Lawn Care/Snow Removal | | | | | |
| Property Taxes | | | | | |
| Homeowner's Insurance | | | | | |
| **Clothing** | | | | | |
| Purchases | | | | | |
| Cleaning/Repair/Alterations | | | | | |
| **Medical** | | | | | |
| Health, Dental, Vision Insurance | | | | | |
| Doctor/Dentist | | | | | |
| Glasses/Contact Lens | | | | | |
| Prescriptions | | | | | |

| Expenses for (Month) (Year) | | | | | |
|---|---|---|---|---|---|
| Expense Categories | Expenditures | | | | |
| **Transportation** | | | | | |
| Car Payments, Lease | | | | | |
| Gas | | | | | |
| Repairs/Maintenance | | | | | |
| Parking | | | | | |
| Bus/Taxi | | | | | |
| **Entertainment** | | | | | |
| Tickets | | | | | |
| Parties Hosted | | | | | |
| Sports Equipment | | | | | |
| Hobby Expenses | | | | | |
| Travel | | | | | |
| **Education** | | | | | |
| Tuition | | | | | |
| Books | | | | | |
| **Miscellaneous** | | | | | |
| Dues for Clubs and Organizations | | | | | |
| Charitable Contributions | | | | | |
| Hair Stylist, Personal Grooming Services | | | | | |
| Other | | | | | |
| | | | | | |
| | | | | | |
| Total Expenses for Month | | | | | |

Now compare your list of historical expenditures to a new list of what you reasonably expect your expenses to be for yourself and any dependent children going forward. Your projected budget will likely be somewhat less than it was during your marriage, but certainly not reduced by half unless you plan to make drastic changes.

If your monthly financial expenditures have been significantly higher than your projected monthly income, you will need to consider ways of either reducing your expenses or increasing your income. One fairly obvious choice is to sell all vehicles other than the one you use most often. Vehicles cost money to maintain and depreciate in value very quickly. If there are loans or leases on the vehicles, you will need to work with the lender to be able to sell the vehicles or return them to the lessor. There may be a cost to do this, so weigh whether or not getting rid of the vehicles will really help reduce monthly expenses.

While I recommend waiting for a year or so to decide about selling a house or moving, sometimes the cost of living in your current home—particularly if there is a large mortgage—makes it impossible to stay in your marital home. Read Chapter 11 for a more detailed discussion about selling a home. If you are renting, read your lease to find out when it expires. If you simply cannot afford the rent, contact the landlord and explain the situation. A sympathetic landlord may release you from any obligations to continue the lease, but do not count on this. It is possible that you could incur expenses for vacating a rental property early.

You can reduce your monthly expenses in other ways too; for example, by not traveling, giving up expensive hobbies or club memberships, reducing charitable contributions, and forgoing paid housekeepers and lawn care. It may become apparent, though, that it will be helpful or even absolutely necessary for you to return to the workforce or switch to a career that will allow you to earn more money.

# § 9.4 Credit

## § 9.4.1 Notifying Creditors of Spouse's Death

You should give your spouse's creditors written notice of his or her death, and you should close any credit card accounts in your spouse's sole name. If there is a balance due, the account will stay open until it is paid off or discharged, but the credit card issuer should be given written notice that the credit card holder is deceased and that any future charges on the card will be fraudulent. You may be able to keep joint credit card accounts open; check your card agreement. If you keep a joint account open, the lender may reduce your credit limit. The lender will also continue to report account activity under your spouse's Social Security number. Issues regarding creditors' claims are discussed in more detail in Chapter 6.

Be aware that some credit card accounts have life insurance that will pay off some or all of the balance if the cardholder dies. If the credit card company is not aware of the death, they will not notify you of the insurance coverage. Some credit card accounts provide life insurance for travel-related accidental deaths if the tickets were purchased with that credit card; you will want to inquire about this coverage if your spouse died in such an accident.

Under federal law, you will not have to requalify for the mortgage on your home, but you may need to reapply and requalify for other kinds of credit as a single borrower.

## § 9.4.2 Review Your Credit Report

There are three major credit reporting companies in the United States: Equifax, Experian, and TransUnion. Credit bureaus collect information in four areas on individuals, which is used by lenders to determine whether or not to extend credit to an applicant and at what interest rate. Information is collected in the following categories:

1. Identifying information including name, address, date of birth, and Social Security number;

2. Existing loan information for current and past loans of all kinds;

3. Inquiries made for credit; and

4. Public record information, such as foreclosure, tax liens, judgments, and bankruptcies.

As of December 1, 2004, federal law gives all Colorado residents the right to obtain a free credit report from each of the three major credit bureaus each year. The report must be sent to you within 15 days of a written or phone request; the reports are also available immediately online. Free annual credit reports can be obtained from:

- Equifax at 800-685-1111; P.O. Box 740241, Atlanta, GA 30374; or www.equifax.com

- Experian at 888-397-3742; P.O. Box 2104, Allen, TX 75013; or www.experian.com

- TransUnion at 800-916-8800; P.O. Box 2000, Chester, PA 19022; or www.transunion.com

- Federal Trade Commission at 877-322-8228; Annual Credit Report Request Service, P.O. Box 105281, Atlanta, GA 30348-5281; or www.ftc.gov or www.annualcreditreport.com

Credit reports list your borrowing activity history and show who has inquired about extending credit to you. Based on the information in credit reports, lenders give borrowers a credit score referred to as a "FICO score." In the past, only lenders could learn a person's FICO score; but now, consumers can learn their scores from a website at www.myfico.com. There is a fee to learn your score. A high score, indicating a good credit rating, makes it easier to borrow money and usually results in offers of credit at lower interest rates. The website contains information on how scores are determined and how consumers can improve their scores.

## § 9.4.3 Apply for Credit in Your Own Name

A good credit rating is very helpful in life. Many married women have never borrowed money individually based on their individual earnings and assets. If you are one of these women, consider applying for a low-balance bank credit card and paying it promptly each month to establish an individual credit record. It is likely that you may need or want to qualify for a reduced-rate mortgage, buy a new car with a loan, or borrow money for some other prudent purpose in the future, and it will be much easier to do so if you have a good credit record and rating. You should also change the account name on your account with utilities, telephone companies, and insurance companies to make it clear that you are now paying the bills and building your own good credit history.

# CHAPTER 10
# VEHICLES

## § 10.1 How Many Vehicles Do You Need?

Many couples have two or more vehicles (including sports cars, sport utility vehicles, trucks, boats, and motorcycles), as well as conventional cars of all kinds. Perhaps your spouse collected them as a hobby or perhaps they were used in a favorite pastime such as fishing or hunting. Unlike some other kinds of personal property, a vehicle can be more of a liability than an asset. The resale value of vehicles depreciates quite rapidly regardless of their condition, although condition is certainly a factor. Vehicles cost money for licensing, insurance, storage, and maintenance. They are a temptation for thieves. Unused vehicles that just sit on the street quickly take on a shabby and run-down look, which does not contribute to the attractiveness of the neighborhood or the property value of your home. While it can be emotionally difficult to sell or dispose of a vehicle your spouse enjoyed, I recommend realistically assessing your transportation needs.

Very few individuals drive more than one vehicle consistently. What many people really need is one reliable vehicle. If you notice after a few months that you are not using more than one vehicle, you should consider selling the rest (and eliminating the costs of maintaining them). The sales proceeds now will almost always be greater than they will be a few years from now.

Alternatively, perhaps other family members could use the vehicles and would enjoy having them. This is particularly true for recreational vehicles. For example, if your spouse enjoyed fishing but you don't (and do not intend to take it up), why not sell the boat or give it to a fellow fishing enthusiast rather than deal with a large space-consuming item you are not using and almost certainly never will? Many widows are not knowledgeable about vehicle maintenance and repairs and feel safer selling all the vehicles and buying a new one in hopes that there will not be major mechanical problems in the near future.

Do not, however, simply give away vehicles immediately after your spouse's death. You may later realize that you would have liked to keep a particular vehicle or that being able to sell it or trade it in would have helped you buy a better car for yourself. You should also remember that if other people are beneficiaries of your spouse's estate, you may need to sell the vehicles and add the proceeds to the estate. Or, the vehicles may have been left to other people in a will or other estate planning instrument you may not yet be aware of.

Colorado permits people to leave vehicles to specific individuals by means of a Memorandum of Disposition of Tangible Personal Property. This is a signed, dated, written list directing to whom items of tangible personal property (including vehicles) are to be distributed on death. If your spouse left a Memorandum stating to whom vehicles are to be given, you can proceed to transfer title to those people and give them the vehicles to do with as they please. If someone tells you that your spouse "promised" to leave them the vehicle, you are not bound by this kind of a statement unless it is also documented by written estate planning documents or is part of an intestate probate estate in which other people are heirs with rights.

To transfer a vehicle title from a decedent to someone else, you will need the original title document. If you cannot find it after a reasonably diligent search, it is possible to get a replacement title through the Department of Motor Vehicles.

Transfer of title usually requires a trip to the Department of Motor Vehicles office. Call the DMV first to find out what you need to bring with you to accomplish the title transfer. If the vehicle was held in joint tenancy between you and your spouse, you will likely just need a state-certified copy of the death certificate. If the vehicle was owned by the two of you as tenants in common or if it was owned by your spouse alone, you will need a death certificate and one of the following: Letters Testamentary, Letters of Administration, or an Affidavit for Collection. The Colorado Department of Motor Vehicles maintains an informative website, including forms, at www.dmv.org/co-colorado/department-motor-vehicles.php.

## § 10.2 Terminating a Lease for a Vehicle

If your spouse leased a vehicle, contact the leasing company relatively soon to find out the options for either terminating the lease due to the death or continuing it in your own name.

## § 10.3 Maintaining Vehicle Insurance

Automobile insurance coverage is crucial to your financial well-being. Auto policies insure both drivers and vehicles against several kinds of risk. Colorado has had both "fault" and "no-fault" auto insurance laws over the years. Car owners are required by law to have auto insurance and to have evidence of the coverage in the car. If a driver is cited for some other kind of violation, the failure to provide proof of currently effective insurance is an additional violation. Even if auto insurance were not mandatory, it would be foolhardy to drive without it.

Auto insurance policies have different components:

- Liability coverage provides insurance for damage to people and property in the event that you are involved in an accident. There are various limits on coverage available for both physical injury and property damage.

- Collision coverage pays for damage caused to your car by a collision. Some people who own older vehicles choose to reduce the amount of collision coverage to reduce their premiums (on the theory that an older vehicle would not be worth repairing if it is seriously damaged).

- Comprehensive insurance covers other kinds of damage to a vehicle, such as hail damage, theft, and vandalism. It also insures sound systems.

Auto insurance also covers medical costs for the driver, passengers, and pedestrians injured in accidents.

This kind of insurance policy has deductibles for the different kinds of coverage. Having a deductible means that the insured person pays the first part of any insured cost up to a stated amount. For example, having a $500 deductible to comprehensive coverage would mean that the insured person would pay the first $500 of a $2,000 bill to repair hail damage, and the insurance company would pay the remaining $1,500. Premiums are usually less if the deductibles are higher.

Some insurance companies offer discounts on premiums if you insure more than one vehicle with them. Some drivers, such as men under age 25, have higher premiums than other groups of people simply because that group statistically has more accidents than others. If you have teenage drivers, it may be possible to get a discount if they have good grades. It can be less expensive to pay the premiums annually or semiannually than monthly.

You should familiarize yourself with your auto insurance sooner rather than later. Do not ignore auto insurance bills. You may want to change to a different auto insurance company than the one your spouse used; sometimes people get in a habit of using one company, while another might offer improved features your spouse was not aware of.

## § 10.4 Vehicle Maintenance

Cars require more than gas. If you were not the spouse responsible for car maintenance, you will need to educate yourself about it to a certain extent if you are going to be a driver from now on. You will want to find an honest and competent repair and maintenance provider and work with that person to set up a schedule for regular maintenance. I recommend keeping a small paper calendar in the car to keep track of what services were performed on which dates and when those services need to be repeated.

## § 10.5 Accidents

If you are involved in a vehicle accident of any kind, call the police and report it. Insurance companies may require you to make a police report before they will cover the damage. You are also legally required to report the event, which sometimes will have criminal issues involved. You do not have to admit fault for anything that happened and should seek the help of an attorney who practices in the area of auto accidents unless the accident was fairly minor and there were no injuries.

## § 10.6 Summary

Unlike many other kinds of assets, vehicles depreciate in value every day. They also cost money to maintain and insure. You are at risk for legal liability if you keep uninsured vehicles and one of them is stolen. After a few months, you should be able to make a realistic assessment of your transportation needs. If your spouse owned vehicles of any kind that you are not using and if the vehicles are left to you under the estate plan or by intestacy, take steps to sell them or even give them to charity in order to reduce your risk of liability if the vehicle is stolen, to reduce your expenses, and to produce cash if there is a sale. Vehicle leases can often be terminated upon a death. Be sure to verify whether or not your spouse bequeathed a vehicle to someone else in a will, memorandum of disposition of tangible personal property, or otherwise.

# CHAPTER 11
# HOME OWNERSHIP
# AND CHANGE IN RESIDENCE

## § 11.1 The Importance of Maintaining Homeowner's (or Renter's) Insurance

Many people are not aware that homeowner's insurance provides coverage for many types of legal problems as well as for damage to a home. These include personal injuries to people on your property and sometimes injuries caused elsewhere by a homeowner's negligence.

Homeowner's insurance premiums are one of the expenses that you really must manage to pay as a priority. If you have a mortgage, these premiums are often automatically paid through your mortgage payments. If you do not have a mortgage, they must be paid separately. Your spouse may have had the premiums deducted automatically from a bank account. If it is not clear to you whether or not this will continue to happen, you need to investigate or ask someone else to help you find out who the homeowner's insurance company is and how the premiums can now be paid. It is very important not to have a gap in coverage. Many homeowner's insurance companies will refuse to continue providing coverage after the death of a homeowner unless the ownership of the home is transferred to a living person within a fairly short period of time.

Renter's insurance does not insure the structure of a home or apartment but does insure the contents and is very important if you are a renter. The last thing you need at this time in your life is to have an uninsured property loss.

Homeowner's insurance policies insure against many kinds of risks of harm relating to ownership of property, including damage caused by the negligence of the homeowner. There are significant differences in the kinds and amounts of coverage. You must have specific coverage for certain luxury items such as jewelry and furs. These items will need to be appraised by specialized appraisers to obtain this coverage.

It is vitally important to report any event that could be covered by a home-owner's policy promptly and in writing to the insurance company. Keep a copy of your letter as proof of prompt notification. Some policies will not provide coverage if they are not notified within a certain period of time. Part of your coverage will be that the insurance company will provide you with an attorney in many situations and will pay the attorney fees. The company will choose the attorney for you from a group of attorneys with whom it has existing contracts to represent its insureds.

Homeowner's insurance typically has a deductible for property damage. This means that you will pay the first part of the costs of repair to your home. The deductible is different for different policies; you will need to read your policy to find out what it is in your case. Sometimes the cost of repair is less than the deductible and the homeowner pays the entire cost of repair.

When you report damage to an insurance company, it will send an adjuster to inspect the damage and then will tell you what it will pay you. If you accept the offer, you will be required to sign a release and agree that you have been fully compensated for the damage. I have heard a number of reports in the last few years that homeowners have had their coverage cancelled by the company at the next renewal after they made a claim for damage to a home. You should find a reputable homeowner's insurance broker and ask for a thorough explanation of your coverage and what features might be preferable for you.

## § 11.2 Changing Ownership of the Home to Your Own Name

If you are not going to sell your home soon after your spouse's death, and you and your legal and financial advisors agree, then you should probably transfer title (*i.e.*, ownership) of the home into your name alone.

If you and your spouse owned your home in joint tenancy, the ownership passes to you by operation of law when your spouse dies. All that must be done to clear title into your sole name is to record a certified copy of your spouse's death certificate in the clerk and recorder's office in the county where the home is located. It is very typical for married couples to take title as joint tenants when they buy a home, and most title insurance companies assume that they will do so, although they do ask your preference.

For a home in Colorado to be owned in joint tenancy, the words "as joint tenants" or "in joint tenancy" must appear on the deed itself. You (or your attorney) will need to carefully read the deed to make sure this is the case. If you do not have the original deed or a photocopy of it, you can get one from the county clerk and recorder's office or the title insurance company that provided you with title insurance when you bought the home. You must also read the deed very carefully to see if the way your spouse's name appears on the deed exactly matches the way it appears on the death certificate. If they are not exactly the same, you will need to record a special form of name affidavit verifying that "John P. Smith" is the same person as "John Paul Smith." Attorneys typically help their clients with all of these tasks, but some people do it on their own.

If you and your attorney determine that your home is owned by you and your deceased spouse, but not in joint tenancy, you will need to record a special form of deed known as a "Personal Representative's Deed of Distribution." These are most often prepared by attorneys because they recite some information about your spouse's probate proceeding. The Personal Representative must sign the deed. A court-certified copy of the Letters of Administration or Letters Testamentary must be recorded with the Personal Representative's Deed.

If your spouse owned the home in his or her sole name, the will or the laws of intestacy will determine whether or not you can take ownership of the home. Unless you are the sole beneficiary of your spouse's estate, you should be sure to discuss this issue with your attorney. Sometimes, particularly in a second or subsequent marriage, the house does not pass to the surviving spouse. It may be held in a trust that gives the spouse the right to live in it for a period of time or for life, but absolute ownership never transfers to the surviving spouse.

If your spouse owned real estate in his or her sole name or with you or someone else as tenants in common (*i.e.*, not joint tenancy), then a probate proceeding will be necessary to transfer title even if it is not required for any other reason.

## § 11.3 Deciding to Keep or Sell Your Home

If you have determined for certain that you do own your home outright, you can decide to stay in the home or to sell it and move. I highly recommend deferring the decision to sell a house for at least a year after a spouse's death. Moving is extremely stressful, and you are not thinking as clearly as you may believe you are soon after a spouse's death. People sometimes believe that their grief will be lessened if they move away from a home filled with reminders of their spouse. Unfortunately, there is no simple way to "forget" your loss, no matter where you are. I am convinced that people make better business decisions about what to do with a home after considerable time has passed, and that it is comforting to stay in familiar surroundings and not to increase stress to your life by adding the moving process at a time already filled with stress.

There are times, however, when the home must be sold soon because the loss of a spouse's income and the economic circumstances of the widowed person make it impossible to keep paying the housing costs. The following comments apply to this situation and also to those of you who have let some time pass and have determined that you really do want to move because a home is too big, takes too much of your disposable income to maintain, no longer suits your needs because of design, or other carefully considered reasons.

## § 11.4 How to Sell a Home

Unless you have sold a home recently and were very involved in the sale, you may not know how to start the process. Some people sell their homes themselves by advertising in the newspaper or simply by letting their friends and neighbors know they want to sell. Perhaps you even know someone who has admired your home and asked to be contacted if you are ever interested in selling.

Many widows are uncomfortable selling a home by themselves, for a number of reasons. There are, unfortunately, knowledgeable people who make offers to purchase property from a widowed person at a price that is far below what the market would bring, on the assumption that the seller is unsophisticated or unaware of how much the value of the home has appreciated since the couple bought it many years ago. It is often hard to know how much to ask for a home without the advice of a broker who deals in homes in the area regularly and keeps informed about recent sales of comparable homes in the area.

Safety is another concern. If you simply place an ad in the newspaper, then you have no idea who may arrive on your doorstep and want to come into your home. People who would never consider letting complete strangers into their homes under any other circumstance sometimes do so when selling a home. There have unfortunately been some serious property crimes and crimes of violence perpetrated by people posing as home buyers. While this is still possible if you have a real estate agent listing and selling your home, it is far less likely since an agent will accompany any buyers who want to see your home. Some sellers who are very concerned with safety ask that their agent and any potential buyer's agent both be present at all showings.

Real estate brokers are also able to help with the contract and title insurance process. If you sell your home yourself, you will likely need your attorney to assist you with these issues unless you are an experienced and knowledgeable seller of real estate.

## § 11.4.1 Selecting an Agent; How Agents Are Paid

Selling your home through a real estate brokerage gives you expertise and market visibility. Real estate brokerages typically have all the agents in the office tour all of the homes listed by anyone in the office. This broadens the scope of people familiar with your home who are likely to be working with current buyers.

In Colorado, real estate agents are licensed by a state agency and must pass an initial licensing exam and take continuing education classes. They may, if they wish, also take a higher-level "broker's exam" to earn that professional designation. The term "Realtor" indicates that an agent is a member of the National Association of Realtors, a trade group.

Real estate agents are paid a commission fee at the closing of the sale of a home. If the house never sells, the agent is not paid. Commissions are based on a percentage of the actual sale price, and they are not set by law. In Colorado, commissions are typically six or seven percent, but are sometimes lower.

A good agent will be very familiar with your neighborhood and the prices for recent actual sales of comparable homes. He or she should be able to advise you frankly about the features of your home that make it attractive and desirable (or less desirable) to buyers. All of these factors bear on what price to initially ask for a home. Some agents suggest very high prices initially, with the idea that the price can be reduced substantially later. While everyone wants to sell their home for as much as possible, listing a home for an extremely high price in comparison with comparable homes in the area likely will result in more time on the market and large price reductions later. You should not necessarily hire the agent who suggests the highest listing price. Some agents do this as a marketing tool and then reduce the price fairly quickly. Pricing a home is not an exact science, but a home that is priced vastly higher than comparable homes in the area is likely to sit on the market without an offer for a long time unless there is something extraordinarily appealing and different about the property.

How do you choose a real estate agent you will be happy with? Many people simply ask people they know to recommend someone with whom they have had a good experience. You might ask your attorney, banker, or accountant for recommendations. You might have an agent you have worked with before or know one socially. If someone recommends an agent to you, ask detailed questions about why the person is recommending the agent. Certain factors are important to some people and not others.

You should of course feel comfortable with the agent's personality and have confidence in his or her ethics and ability. You should ask the agent for a market analysis of the value of your home and explore in-depth with the agent the factors considered in the analysis. Ask about the proposed marketing plan, including listing in the Multiple Listing Service (MLS), newspapers, and on the Internet. Some sellers want open houses, where the public can come into the home and tour it, but other sellers object to them. Many experienced agents do not believe that open houses are effective in actually selling homes, because many of the people who tour the home cannot afford to buy it, are just interested in seeing decorating ideas, or are not serious buyers for some other reason.

The agent may make some suggestions about things that should be done to your home to get it ready to sell. The agent is not trying to insult your home, but buyers can be put off by certain features of a home. You may be asked to clean out basements and closets and to generally reduce clutter. You might consider renting a storage facility for a short time and moving non-essential items into it to give your home a roomier look. If it has been quite a while since you last moved, it may be time to get rid of things you don't really use and to either have a garage sale or give items away to family or charities. Your agent may suggest painting the home inside or outside (or both) in neutral colors to appeal to a broad number of people. If the carpet is in very bad condition, you might want to re-carpet (also in a neutral color). Some agents suggest that pets be sent to live with a friend or relative during the sales process. The house should be kept very clean and tidy.

If you interview a potential listing agent who you do not feel comfortable with for some reason, interview one or two more, possibly from different agencies, and then compare them.

## § 11.4.2 Listing Agreements

When you choose a listing agent, you will be asked to sign a listing agreement. There are two basic kinds of listing agreements, but the one most commonly used is called an "Exclusive Right to Sell Contract." With this kind of agreement, the listing agent will be paid a commission, as described in the agreement, regardless of who buys the property. The other kind of listing contract is called an "Exclusive Agency" agreement, under which the listing broker is not paid if you find a buyer yourself without any agent's involvement.

Sometimes sellers and listing agents use an Exclusive Right to Sell contract with an exclusion for a certain potential buyer for a short period. Perhaps an acquaintance of the seller is interested in a possible purchase but has not made an offer or a decision. The seller wants to move along on a sale, but feels that a commission is not due in this circumstance if the acquaintance ends up buying the home. If this is your situation, discuss it with a potential listing broker. He or she should be willing to accommodate you for a fairly short period of time, and listing the home for sale with an exclusion for one particular buyer may nudge your interested party into making a decision one way or another.

You should be aware that Colorado currently has three forms of agency relationships: (1) seller's agents, (2) buyer's agents, and (3) so-called transaction agents. Buyer's agents clearly represent the buyer. Transaction agents represent the "transaction," which I believe can result in divided loyalty that could work against either the buyer or seller. If you are a seller, I strongly recommend that you hire an agent as a seller's agent and not as a transaction agent. You should have an agent whose legal and ethical duty is to you alone.

## § 11.4.3 Timing the Sale

Agents have differing opinions on the best time of year to list a house for sale. Individual factors about you, your neighborhood, and your home will bear on this. Many families with children like to move in the summer, but this certainly is not universal. Discuss this issue with your agent. Many agents believe that January through May are ideal months to initially list a home for sale.

## § 11.4.4 Will You Have to Pay Tax on the Sale of Your Home?

Many people who have not sold a home for a long time do not realize that it is possible to owe capital gains tax on the sale of a home. Under the tax law prior to 1997, it was possible to defer paying tax on the sale of a home into the future indefinitely if the seller purchased a replacement residence of equal or greater value within a specific time. There was a one-time exemption of $125,000 of capital gain for sellers over age 55.

The law currently in effect is different. Now, each individual can receive up to $250,000 of capital gain (profit) on the sale of a home without owing any tax, provided that the seller owned and occupied the residence for at least two of the previous five years before the sale. The amount of gain is calculated on how much the sales proceeds exceed the seller's "tax basis," i.e., what was paid for the home. Married couples can exclude up to $500,000 of capital gain. Your deceased spouse's interest in the home receives a new tax basis of its date-of-death value due to a section of the tax law that gives all assets owned by decedents a new tax basis at death. Many people can sell homes without any capital gains tax and without the requirement that they buy a new residence of equal or greater value. Some people have lived in their homes for many years and the value has appreciated more than these exemption amounts. This is an important factor in deciding whether or not to sell your home. You and your attorney and accountant should determine clearly whether or not capital gains tax will be due on the sale of your home before deciding to sell it.

# CHAPTER 12
# CHILDREN

---

## § 12.1 Support for Grieving Children

The purpose of this chapter is to discuss support for children younger than age 19 who have had a parent die. Children 19 and older are still profoundly affected by the death of a parent but are, in many ways, adults with the same reaction older people have toward the death of a parent.

### § 12.1.1 Preschool Children

Preschool-aged children have a very limited understanding of death. They generally do not yet understand that death is universal and does not just happen to bad people. They have trouble with the concept that death is permanent and irreversible.

In explaining the death of a parent to a child, it is helpful to be quick and honest. Do not try to wait for the "perfect time." It would be unfortunate and undesirable for a child to accidentally overhear other people talking about a parent's death or to hear the news from someone other than the surviving parent. With preschool children, you should use only one word for "dead." You should explain what death means, *e.g.*, that the person can no longer eat, breathe, come home, etc. You may need to repeat these concepts over and over. It is crucially important for your future relationship with your children to be honest with them regardless of how young they are. A child should never be told that a parent has left on a trip or is asleep. Euphemisms are confusing for children.

When telling a child that a parent has died, touch the child. Reassure the child that the parent loved them and that it is unlikely that anyone else they know will die soon. This is a common fear in children who have lost a parent, since having a parent die is one of the most profound losses in life and causes children to understand, usually for the first time, that death can happen to anyone at any time, not just to very elderly people or to "other people." A child whose parent has died often develops a great fear that the surviving parent will also die. You should encourage your children to express their feelings regardless of what they are and reassure them that it is okay to grieve, cry, laugh, or express any other feelings that they have.

As a surviving parent, you must realize that there are no magic words that will comfort your child. It is not helpful to say to a child "I know how you feel." It is also not helpful to tell a child that God took the parent because God loved the parent so much; this explanation can cause children to develop a concept of God as cruel and unfeeling. Children need to be reassured that they had nothing to do with the parent's death and that there was nothing they could have done to prevent it.

## § 12.1.2 School-Age Children

The advice for preschool-age children also applies to school-age children. School-age children are capable of having more mature understandings of the ramifications of death, but they often believe that death only happens to very old people or to people outside their own families.

## § 12.1.3 Children Ages 13 Through 18

Children in this age group understand intellectually that death is irreversible, universal, and inevitable. Adolescent culture, however, often romanticizes death from fast driving, drugs, and other risky behavior and fosters a concept of challenging death by dangerous activities.

Adolescents have a habit of distancing themselves from adults under the most normal circumstances. It helps to remember that the function of adolescence is separation from the nuclear family, the development of an independent life, and the completion of developmental tasks for young people to become functional adults. Adolescents typically are preoccupied with themselves, and the developmental task central to healthy adolescence is mastery and competence in dealing with the challenges of life as an adult. Adolescents are in the process of establishing a stable identity for themselves and defining who they are.

It is crucial when dealing with adolescents to do everything possible to reestablish communication and intimacy. Even if adolescents are unwilling to talk to adults, it is the responsibility of adults to keep the lines of communication open and to make every effort to know about adolescents' lives despite their own typical efforts to keep parents and other adults out of certain areas.

Peers are terribly important to adolescents, who often seek guidance from each other on emotionally powerful issues. The peers of an adolescent suffering from the death of a parent are not likely to know very much about death or grief. Support groups can offer a peer group that has the experience of the death of a parent in common. Since adolescence is a time when young people want to be like everyone else, the death of a parent can create feelings of shame because this event makes them very different from everyone else. A peer support group can offer adolescents a safe place to talk about feelings without feeling "different."

## § 12.1.4 Stages of Grief in Children

As with adults, children experience a brief, intense period of initial sadness we call grief. They then move beyond the initial stage of shock into the process of mourning, which ends only when the loss of a parent is incorporated into the child's life. The stages include sadness, denial, guilt, anger, shame or stigma, and finally acceptance. Children of all ages are vulnerable to feeling odd and different in a society when most young people have two living parents, whether or not the children live in a nuclear family setting.

The mourning process is repeated in successive developmental phases as the child grows older, and can re-emerge repeatedly to be recycled at milestones in a child's life—such as graduations, weddings, and when the child has his or her own children. It is very important to reminisce about the dead parent; this is particularly important for children who are the same gender as the deceased parent.

Children whose parent has died often feel guilt for not being able to prevent the death of the parent or for contributing to the parent's death. Children often fantasize that they have control over what happens in the world, and believe that if they had behaved differently at a certain time or in a certain circumstance, perhaps the parent's death could have been avoided.

Children often react with anger to a parent's death. Anger can be a response not only to the injustice of losing the parent and to the perceived cause of the death, but also to all of the upset adults surrounding the child. In addition, adults in the child's life who are themselves upset are often less patient and tolerant of children's behavior. Some experts believe that anger can be a symptom of depression, particularly in males, who are acculturated to express anger more freely than sadness. True feelings of acceptance often are not achieved until the child becomes an adult.

# § 12.2 Single Parenting

## § 12.2.1 Reestablishing Routines and Family Structure

It is important to explain to children, immediately after they are told that a parent has died, what will change about their lives and what will not change. In general, the less change to a child's routine, the better. It helps children to know that their daily routine, school schedules, activities, vacation plans, etc. will continue just as in the past. They should be told that holidays will still be celebrated, that the surviving parent will attend parent night at school, and that they will continue to participate in sports, scouting, music, and other activities in which they have been involved.

Many people who are newly widowed have a tendency to want to make big changes in their lives and their daily routines, in a futile effort to escape the pain they feel. Change adds an additional level of stress to children and should be avoided as much as possible. Peace, happiness, and equilibrium cannot be restored to life by making external changes such as moving to a new location or changing jobs. Coping with the death of a parent reduces the ability of a child to cope with other stressors; so to the greatest extent possible, children should not be required to deal with other stressors at this time in their lives.

It is helpful for the family to decide on a uniform approach they can use in response to unsettling events such as telephone calls asking for the deceased parent and questions from other people asking how the child is doing. It can be helpful, at least for a few days, to have a friend or relative answer the home phone until relatives, friends, acquaintances, and coworkers are notified of the death. It is often difficult for children to know how to respond to well-meaning adults who ask them how they are doing. It is helpful for children to make a plan for responses to this kind of question with a stock answer such as, "Thank you for your concern; we're dong okay."

### § 12.2.2 Your Children's Needs and Your Own Needs

Unfortunately for surviving parents, your children need you to be thinking clearly at a time when you are grief-stricken and need nurturing yourself. Your reactions to your children at this vulnerable time in their lives will impact them forever. With older children, it is sometimes tempting to rely on them and make them into a "little father" or "little mother" of the family in the place of the deceased spouse. This is terribly unfair to children. As adults, widowed persons need to recognize their own need for support and to obtain it from other adults. It is important for both the surviving parent and the children to create a safe and peaceful home environment. Neither the parent nor the children should be rushed or pushed through the stages of mourning.

### § 12.2.3 Sources of Help and Support

The most obvious source of help and support for a newly widowed person with children is the extended family. In our mobile society, extended family may not live in the same area as the survivors. In that case, close family friends often step in and act as surrogate extended family members. The ongoing involvement of relatives or of close family friends on a regular basis can make a life-changing difference to children who have lost a parent, as well as to a grieving widowed parent. Our culture sometimes makes us feel that we need to be independent and self-sufficient in all ways. In cases where a parent has died leaving young children, however, one of the most important things the surviving parent can do is to encourage and build an ongoing matrix of support.

## § 12.3 Stepchildren

### § 12.3.1 Maintaining a Relationship

If your stepchildren have lived with you most of the time, all of the recommendations made above regarding children apply to your situation. If your stepchildren do not live with you most of the time, but have spent significant amounts of time with you, then you, they, or their other natural parent may believe that the death has terminated any reason for your relationship with your stepchildren. However, it can be very helpful for stepchildren who have had a good relationship with the stepparent to continue it. It is likely to be the responsibility of the newly widowed person to make the effort to continue the relationship. In general, children do best with as many supportive adults in their lives as possible, and it can cause them great pain to lose the affection of a stepparent as well as losing their parent.

## § 12.3.2 Avoiding Financial Conflicts

Ideally, the deceased parent had done thoughtful estate planning to avoid financial conflict between you, as a surviving spouse, and your stepchildren. If your spouse was paying court-ordered child support, that obligation is likely to continue despite the death of your spouse. This can come as a surprise to a surviving spouse.

It is common in separation agreements in a divorce for a court to order both parents to carry life insurance to replace court-ordered child support in the event of the death of a parent during a child's minority. If this is the case, the issue may already be taken care of. If your deceased spouse was ordered to provide life insurance and did not do so, or if he or she was not ordered to do so, you should expect a claim against your deceased spouse's estate for child support and possibly contribution toward college tuition. If this happens, you should consult an attorney experienced in family law and possibly a financial planner and/or expert accountant to assist you and your stepchildren and their other parent in working through a method of providing for the children while providing for you as a surviving spouse.

When stepchildren are adults, the issue of inheritance from a deceased parent who is survived by the child's stepparent can become hostile and negative. The adult stepchildren may believe that their deceased parent's estate should pass to them and can resent what passes to a surviving spouse, particularly if the surviving stepparent is considerably younger than the deceased parent. Once again, good estate planning can minimize these issues;

but if you are newly widowed and the stepparent of adult stepchildren, you may want to work with your advisors to develop a plan for coping with these issues if they arise.

# CHAPTER 13
# STARTING, RESUMING,
# OR CHANGING CAREERS

## § 13.1 Pros and Cons

If you were working at the time of your spouse's death, you should not make any decisions for a number of months about retiring, changing jobs or careers, or anything else related to your career that you can reasonably defer. Even if you were planning to retire in the near future before your spouse's death, I would advise you to defer the final decision for a period of time. Many people find that retirement brings new and unexpected stresses, including a loss of identity from a career as well as loneliness and isolation. Retirement may have seemed like something to look forward to with a spouse, but as a widowed person it may not offer the same advantages, at least for a while. Now is not the time to add to the sources of stress in your life. Many people feel that they simply cannot face returning to their job after the death of a spouse; however, work can add a sense of normalcy to life, which can be helpful emotionally.

If you are younger than retirement age but have been a full-time home-maker, you might find yourself either needing to work for financial reasons or wanting to work to add meaning and accomplishment to your life. It may seem overwhelming to think about getting a job for a while; if you can postpone the job search for a few months, you will probably be in a better emotional condition to deal with the challenges this presents.

If you have been out of the workforce for a while, you will face the same challenges every other job applicant faces under those circumstances as well as the emotional pain of losing your spouse. It is sometimes difficult to resume a career you gave up a number of years ago because you may have lost skills or just not kept up with new developments in your field. Sometimes people only need a brief refresher course to step back into a former career. But for many people—not just widowed people—it is challenging to resume a career after a long absence. This in no way means it is impossible, but it may take time and effort to find the right place for you.

Other people may have been out of the workforce for a very long time, never had a career, or simply do not want to resume the kind of work they did in the past. Some widowed people decide to take up an entirely new career or to return to school to gain the education they need for a particular field. Older students typically do well academically because of their maturity, motivation, and focus.

If you have always wondered what it would be like to enter a certain field or regretted that you did not train for it earlier in your life, explore what it would take for you to develop a career in your area of interest. Do not assume that you are necessarily too old to develop a new career. Many colleges and universities have academic counseling centers for older prospective students interested in undergraduate or graduate programs. These centers offer a variety of tests designed to help students understand their interests and abilities. In one case I am familiar with, a widow in her late thirties who had a bachelor's degree in library science consulted an academic counseling center, where it was suggested that she return to school and earn another degree in computer science. She did so and has had a successful career in private industry as a records and information manager for a large international company.

Another possibility is working for a temporary employment agency. Many people get permanent jobs by working with a temporary agency that places them with businesses where there may good fit between the employee's skills and personality and the company's need. Working temporarily for an employer allows you to become familiar with the company environment and the nature of the permanent jobs available there. Be sure you know what kind of jobs the agency fills before signing on. Some agencies focus on clerical help, some on telephone solicitors, and others in technological fields. Be sure the type of work they offer is something appealing to you.

There are many places to find job opportunities. You could consult an employment agency and let them get interviews for you. University placement offices often maintain and share with their alumni lists of employers seeking to fill positions. But the vast majority of people find jobs through friends and acquaintances who know that a person is looking for work. For that reason, if you want to return to work, tell as many people as possible and ask them to let other people know that you are looking.

## § 13.2 Volunteer Work: A Way to Add Meaning to Life

If you are already retired or do not need or want to return to paid work, consider becoming a volunteer for an organization that is important to you. Most of us have a social cause or charitable interest that has true meaning for us. It could be in the area of education, health, religion, child or animal welfare, nature and the environment, alleviation of poverty, abused women, or any number of other causes. I have known retired business people who have volunteered with Junior Achievement and similar programs and have enjoyed helping young people learn about business. Many school systems have programs for parents or other adults to volunteer in the classroom, sometimes as surrogate "grandparents" for the class and in other roles. It often helps to alleviate your grief to get involved in helping to ease the suffering of others or to contribute something positive to the world. You can also join "guilds" or support groups for hospitals or other organizations and make new friends who share your interests. Being a regular volunteer helps bring you back into the world and alleviates isolation. Many people continue to volunteer into very old age.

## § 13.3 Resumes and Job Applications

There are many excellent books on how to prepare a resume. University career centers and employment agencies also help people with resumes. Different factors are stressed in different career fields. I would advise you to find a guide to resume writing that has examples in your career area. Make sure that the spelling and grammar on your resume are perfect. Some employers automatically throw away resumes with misspelled words. Do not be tempted to make any inaccurate statements on your resume; employers are more likely to check references than they once were. After you have put your resume together, ask an intelligent and professional friend to review it for you and make suggestions. Take advantage of any professional career counselors available to you to help with this process.

There are also many reference sources available to advise you on how to apply for a job. In general, do as much research as you can about a prospective employer prior to an interview. Learn what the employer does, where they do it, who their audience is, and who works for them. If possible, find out who will be interviewing you and learn as much as you can about those people. If possible, find a common interest or background you share with them. Many companies have websites that give biographies of employees.

Be ready to explain why you are interested in working for this particular employer, what challenges they face that you could help solve, and what benefits you can bring to them. Learn and use the "vocabulary" of the industry. If you know people in a particular industry, you can often get an "informational" interview even if they are not hiring at that time. Perhaps they can refer you to someone in the same field who is currently looking to hire.

## § 13.4 Starting a Business

You may have often thought about starting a business of your own, and this time in your life feels like the right time to do so. Running your own business is often all-consuming because you are ultimately responsible for every aspect of the business. Many small businesses fail because they are not adequately financed. It is very common for people to underestimate the costs of doing business and the amount of time they will need to work to make the business profitable.

If you think starting a business is for you, then spend a great deal of time planning all aspects of the business and get the help of a good business accountant. If you cannot afford to lose the money you put into the business, you should reconsider the idea. Do as much market research as you can to learn about the prospects for the industry. Some types of businesses simply are not very profitable. It is often a good idea to work for another business in the field to learn how to run the kind of business that interests you before launching your own.

## § 13.5 Summary

You may need or want to continue a career in order to provide for your financial support, to provide a sense of satisfaction or achievement in your life, or to keep you connected with your work colleagues and the outside world.

Even if you were not working before your spouse's death, you may need to seek work for financial reasons or you may want to work for the same non-financial reasons as stated above. If you were already retired at your spouse's death or if you simply do not want or need to join the paid workforce, you should seriously consider becoming a volunteer for one of the many worthy causes available to you in order to make a contribution to the world and to give yourself the satisfaction of helping others while remaining connected with other people.

# CHAPTER 14
# INVESTMENTS

## § 14.1 Investing to Meet Your Current and Future Needs

You may, perhaps for the first time in your life, need to make some decisions about large sums of money—or what might at first seem like large sums of money. You may have received cash from life insurance or the assets of a retirement plan or IRA, and now need to decide how to invest it to meet your goals. You also may still be working and need to develop a greater understanding of investments to direct your own retirement planning through your employment. The purpose of this chapter is to introduce you to some basic concepts of investing and to describe some of the investment opportunities available to you.

By now, you should have gone through the process discussed in Chapter 9 to determine your current and projected future assets, liabilities, and needs. If not, do not begin investing until you have had the opportunity to discuss your financial goals and objectives with the advisors you have chosen or have thoroughly educated yourself on what you need and how to get it.

Some widowed people feel destitute when they are not, while others feel that they can spend freely because they received a large amount of cash all at once (but they are not being realistic about their future needs for basic support). Your emotions might not permit you to have a realistic picture of your future finances without some expert outside help, and you could make decisions you will later regret. In many cases, household income is reduced, sometimes drastically, upon the death of a spouse, so careful planning to invest for current or future income is vital.

Consider your age when creating your investment strategy. The younger you are, the longer your money must last. Also consider your obligations to other dependents. If you need to support children and provide for college, your strategy will be different than that of an older person whose children are financially independent.

## § 14.2 Importance of an Investment Strategy and Diversification

An investment strategy, which likely includes a written investment policy, requires a clear understanding of your financial goals. If you are relatively young and still working, your investment strategy is likely to be to fund your retirement some years in the future as well as to meet current income needs if your earned income without your spouse's income is not adequate to do so. In contrast, if you are now retired and your spouse was retired at death, your needs may be more immediate.

In very simple terms, some investments are designed to produce current income and others to produce future increases in value that will be recognized when the asset is sold. It is unlikely that any one investment will do a good job of attaining both of these investment goals. It is therefore necessary to diversify your investments to take care of current and future needs. Diversification also means investing in different kinds of assets and in different industries and sectors of the economy to try to avoid the risk of loss that is possible if the bulk of a person's money is invested in a concentrated area that does not perform well during a period of time. Many investors with large concentrations of stock in high-tech companies learned a painful lesson about diversification beginning in 2000.

Risk tolerance is part of an investment strategy. Some younger people who are still working may be willing to risk losses in exchange for possible high returns, since they don't depend on their investment income for their current needs and know they can continue to work and recover from a loss in value of an investment. Retired people, by contrast, are often unwilling to risk possible loss in value and will forgo possible future gain in exchange for reduced risk that their investment will actually lose value. Unfortunately, the safest investment options often produce low returns of both income and appreciation and generally do not keep pace with inflation. A person facing a possible long life expectancy in retirement may not be able to invest solely in very "safe" vehicles, such as certificates of deposit, because their return may be so low that they will run out of money after years of inflation at rates higher than the interest rate they are paid by the bank.

Investment strategy generally has three objectives: (1) accumulation of wealth, (2) use of wealth, and (3) estate planning. Investments are best able to accumulate value if they are not needed for current income. Upon retirement, the accumulation function is likely to slow since funds begin to be withdrawn for living expenses. Estate planning includes a strategy to pass value to the next generation at the lowest possible transfer cost. For many people, passing wealth to their heirs may be an emotional desire, but their primary objective should be to take care of their own needs. An investment strategy will determine what percentage of a person's assets will be allocated to the various available investment classes. There is no "one-size-fits-all" strategy that meets everyone's needs.

Investment advisors tell us that once an investment strategy is in place and assets are acquired that comply with the strategy, they must constantly monitor the asset allocation to make sure that changes in sectors in the economy, whether positive or negative, do not skew the percentage of assets in any one class out of the percentage determined in the investment strategy. Remember to include everything you own or have rights to in the planning process. People sometimes forget about retirement plans or fail to take into account the fact that withdrawals are all taxed as ordinary income even if the accounts hold stocks that would be taxed differently if sold in a non-retirement plan account.

# § 14.3 Investment Concepts

The following are some descriptions of basic concepts about investments.

## § 14.3.1 Debt Versus Equity

Debt investments are loans you make to someone else in return for the borrower's promise to pay you interest at a specific or variable rate for a definite period of time. Debt investments include interest-bearing bank accounts, certificates of deposit, bonds of all kinds, notes, mortgages, and treasury instruments of varying kinds. People generally invest in debt instruments to increase their income.

Equity means ownership of something, usually stock in a publicly traded company (in the context of investments).

### § 14.3.2 Liquidity

Liquidity is the ability to convert an investment into cash very quickly. Some investments require that your money be kept in the investment for a specific period of time and cannot be withdrawn without paying a penalty. Lack of liquidity can be a problem in an economic emergency. No one should have all of their assets in illiquid investments or those that require a penalty to be paid for withdrawal before a certain date.

### § 14.3.3 Tax-Free Income

Some investments, generally bonds issued by a government entity, are exempt from federal (and sometimes state) income tax. They produce a lower yield, but the return is not reduced by taxes.

### § 14.3.4 Tax-Deferred Income

Interest and gain in IRAs and retirement plans and some annuities do not incur tax until the money is distributed to the account owner or beneficiary. It can grow tax-free for years. The entire amount of all withdrawals is taxed at ordinary income tax rates, both federal and state.

### § 14.3.5 Capital Gain

Capital gain is the increase in value of a capital asset, such as stock, over its original cost. It is not subject to tax until the asset is sold. Assets held for a year or longer have their gain taxed at a special low rate known as the long-term capital gains rate.

### § 14.3.6 Risk Tolerance

Often, the safest investments pay the lowest returns, while others pay higher returns but carry greater risk that the entire investment could be lost.

## § 14.4 Investment Options

The following are very brief and simple descriptions of some of the characteristics of various investments.

### §14.4.1 Insured Savings Accounts

Money can be deposited in an interest-bearing savings account at a bank, credit union, or savings and loan association insured by the FDIC. Accounts at any one financial institution are insured up to $100,000 per depositor. If you have more than one account at the same institution, the FDIC still only insures $100,000 for all of your accounts combined. Savings accounts typically pay very low rates of interest, but the funds are immediately accessible.

### § 14.4.2 Money Market Funds

These are very liquid interest-bearing accounts that usually invest in short-term government debt instruments. Banks and brokerages offer them.

### § 14.4.3 Insured Certificates of Deposit

A certificate of deposit (CD) is an account where you agree to deposit a certain amount in a bank or other financial institution for a certain period of time for a specified interest rate. There are wide ranges of periods of time available for CDs. As a rule, the longer the term, the higher the interest rate. CDs can also be insured by the FDIC under the same rules as savings accounts. There will be a penalty for early withdrawal. It would be unwise to put most or all of your money in a single long-term CD, since it would be expensive to access the money if you needed it in an emergency. You might, however, consider putting cash from a life insurance policy in a six-month CD while you develop your financial plan for your future. You could also buy several CDs with varying maturity dates.

### § 14.4.4 Treasury Instruments

Treasury bills are U.S. government-guaranteed debt instruments that pay interest. They are sold in $1,000 denominations and can be for 13-week or 26-week terms. Treasury notes are also government-guaranteed. Treasury notes come in $1,000 denominations for periods of two, three, five, or ten years. Treasury Inflation-Protected Securities (TIPS) are also issued by the government, which sets a fixed interest rate on each series of TIPS it sells. The unique feature of TIPS is that the value of the principal is adjusted semiannually based on the Consumer Price Index. Thereafter, interest is applied on the new inflation-adjusted principal. Interest payments therefore rise with inflation; they could also drop with deflation. All of these instruments are commonly used to hold estate funds for relatively short periods during administration of the estate. They can be sold prior to maturity, and can be purchased directly from the government at www.publicdebt.treas.gov/sec/seciis.htm.

## § 14.4.5 Stocks

"Stock" in the context of investing usually refers to shares of corporations publicly traded on a stock exchange. A person who owns stock owns part of the corporation, not its underlying assets. People invest in some stocks to receive stock dividends (income). Many stocks do not pay dividends, but investors buy them in hopes that their value will go up and that they can be sold later for a profit. Shares of publicly traded stock are very liquid and can be sold immediately if there is a need for cash.

## § 14.4.6 Bonds

Bonds issued by any kind of government subdivision are usually referred to as municipal bonds. They pay interest, which is generally tax-free for investors who live in the jurisdiction where the bonds are issued. There are also taxable bonds that are not issued by governmental subdivisions. The federal government also issues savings bonds that accumulate interest for a period of years. Some bonds can be "called," in which case the owner is paid for the bond before the term of the bond expires, at the option of the bond issuer. Some bonds are quite easily liquidated.

## § 14.4.7 Mutual Funds

Mutual funds are investments in which money managers buy a variety of stocks and bonds, and individual investors own a portion of the total "fund." There are many kinds of mutual funds available that focus on certain kinds of investments. Some own just bonds, others own just stocks, and others own a blend. Some mutual funds charge an initial fee, called a "load," while others are "no-load." There are likely to be other fees and charges, though, including a charge when the fund interest is sold. Ask for complete written information on all costs and fees. The fees might seem small, but can add up over time.

Mutual funds are very liquid. They can be a good choice for investors who do not have a large amount to invest but who still want some diversification.

## §14.4.8 Real Estate

There are many ways to invest in real estate. Real estate investments tend to be very illiquid and require a fairly large initial investment, which make it hard to diversify your investments. While your home may be valuable and may greatly increase in value over time, it is not in the same category as other forms of real estate investments since its main function is to provide you with a place to live. Some people own rental houses or apartment houses and rent to tenants to receive rental income and eventually to recognize a profit when they sell the house or building. Others own commercial property such as office buildings, shopping centers, warehouses, etc. Ownership can be (1) direct, (2) through an entity such as a limited partnership, or (3) through a real estate investment trust (REIT), which is an investment vehicle where the public buys an interest in an entity that owns real estate. It is also possible now to invest in "Tenant in Common" (TIC) interests in real estate through companies that market them. TICs are the ownership of a percentage of a building or project and can pay current rental income and later produce gain when sold.

## § 14.4.9 Annuities

There are few investment vehicles as hard to understand as annuities. There are also few investments that generate sales commissions as high as annuities. For this reason, annuities are heavily marketed; seminars are frequently presented to sell consumers on the benefits of annuities. These are often not advertised as seminars on the subject of annuities, but rather as seminars on financial planning or similar topics. In recent years, there has been a trend at banks to encourage customers to purchase annuities with the proceeds of certificates of deposit that have matured. They are often marketed in a high-pressure environment and held out as an ideal financial tool for people who do not know much about investing and do not want to learn about it or deal with an individual financial advisor.

Many financial advisors who do not earn commissions from the sale of financial products consider annuities to be unwise investments for retired people in general, due to the potentially long period of time the assets cannot be accessed without a penalty and the short period of time before the owner might need funds for living expenses in retirement. Unlike IRAs and qualified retirement plans, which make it possible to withdraw as much as you want or need at any time after age 59?, some annuities prohibit withdrawal of funds for a number of years.

More than with many classes of assets, I find a large degree of disappointment with annuities and strong indications that people buy them without a clear understanding of the terms of the contract, the tax effects, the cost of backing out of the whole arrangement, and the imprudence of putting all or a large percentage of a person's assets available for investment into any one vehicle.

In some situations, though, certain types of annuities can be an acceptable option for a portion of an individual's total investments. The term "annuity" really refers to four different kinds of insurance products, with variations among them offered by different providers.

### Tax-Deferred Fixed Annuities

This kind of annuity produces interest income at a specified rate. Unlike some investments, however, the annuity grows in value with the income tax payment deferred until the annuity is cashed out. Be aware, though, that like IRAs and qualified retirement plans, there is a penalty for withdrawal before age 59½. Many people are surprised when they owe income tax at the time of withdrawal, so remember that there will be some tax due after you take money out of an annuity and be sure to plan to have enough money to pay the tax on the withdrawn funds, which may mean withdrawing more than you need for the purpose you need the money for. Consumers should also have clear written statements about the interest rate to be earned by the annuity. Some annuities offer a higher rate in the first year, followed by lower rates in subsequent years.

### Tax-Deferred Variable Rate Annuities

These are tax-deferred vehicles. Critics of these kind of annuities object to the fact that they allow investors to choose only among specified mutual funds and that withdrawals from these annuities are taxed at ordinary income rates, which can be as high as 35 percent federal tax with state income tax added on. In contrast, long-term capital gain and qualifying dividends in regular stock ownership accounts are taxed at long-term capital gains rates, currently at 15 percent maximum, with state tax added on. If, as is likely, however, it is prudent for you to own bonds or interests in a real estate investment trust (REIT), those interest payments will be taxed at ordinary income tax rates in any event. At least if they are held in a tax-deferred variable annuity, the tax will be deferred.

Be aware, however, that this kind of annuity has high annual costs, averaging around 2.3 percent per year. Part of this cost is due to the life insurance that is often offered as part of the annuity contract, which guarantees that the annuity owner's heirs will receive at least some benefit if the investments held in the annuity do not perform well. Independent financial advisors often discourage purchase of tax-deferred variable annuities unless the purchaser has at least a 20-year life expectancy. As to life insurance, you may be able to obtain it at a lower cost for the same death benefit by purchasing standalone life insurance.

While this kind of annuity has benefits in some situations, in general, it is likely to be less expensive to be sure you have invested as much as possible through traditional tax-deferred programs, such as 401(k) plans available through employment, simply because the associated costs can be lower. Some providers, such as TIAA-CREF and Vanguard Group, offer lower cost tax-deferred annuities.

### Immediate Fixed Annuities

These annuities provide an immediate income stream that does not vary. As part of a total financial plan, these contracts can offer a steady and predictable income that the annuity owner cannot outlive. Unlike the other kinds of annuities, immediate fixed annuities can be appropriate for retired people since they immediately begin to receive an income and do not have to wait for a number of years to access their money without a penalty.

One drawback to them—and this can become a major detriment for people who invest too much of their money into this kind of annuity—is that there is no inflation protection. The payments are, as the contract will disclose, set permanently. An income stream that appears adequate today will most certainly not remain so with the passage of time. For this reason, people generally should not put a majority of their liquid assets into an immediate fixed annuity. The other major drawback to these annuities is that unless otherwise provided in the contract, the payments stop on the death of the annuity owner. Thus, the heirs of a person who uses a large sum of money to buy this kind of annuity and then doesn't live very long will likely feel cheated.

### *Immediate Variable Annuities*

This kind of annuity allows the owner to choose from a menu of mutual funds. Rather than getting tax-deferred growth, however, the owner gets immediate income. The amount of income varies according to the amount of the original investment, the age and sex of the person buying the annuity, and the annuity's "performance hurdle" rate. The income rises and falls based on the performance of the mutual funds chosen as compared to the performance hurdle rate. It is possible, but in no way guaranteed, to receive a generous income from this kind of annuity. Be sure to get clear written information about what happens on the death of the owner/annuitant. Some people are under the mistaken impression that something will pass to their children at their death from an annuity, when this is not the case. You may not care about this feature, but should be informed in case you do.

## § 14.5 Learning More

This chapter provides a very elementary overview of investing. It is in your best interests to educate yourself on investing through books, classes, or consultation with an investment advisor. There are also written materials aimed at novice investors. Just remember that no one has found the one investment "secret" that is the perfect answer for everyone.

# CHAPTER 15
# ESTATE PLANNING

## § 15.1 What Is This Process, and Why Do I Have to Think About It Now?

If you have been widowed, you may very well now hold your family's future in your hands. This is not an overstatement of how serious your responsibility is. Depending on how thorough your late spouse's estate planning was, you are likely to have complete or nearly complete control over your assets and the assets you and your spouse acquired during your marriage. If you have minor children, you now have sole decision-making authority over their lives. You are most likely now solely in charge of your own future and solely responsible for what could happen to you if you were to become seriously ill or pass away yourself. This may all add up to a sense of crushing responsibility at a vulnerable time in your life.

You could ignore these facts, abdicate your responsibility in these matters, and simply do nothing. If you think deeply, though, you will realize that by doing nothing, you place your own life and livelihood and that of your children in the hands of others, possibly strangers. You literally give up control of your future and your family's future. In addition (and unfortunately), after a death families often interpret a failure to plan as a lack of caring by the person who died. In reality, a failure to do estate planning is usually a result of discomfort with the subject matter and a lack of sense of urgency more than a lack of caring for the family.

Many people think that they will know "when the time is right" to do their estate planning. People commonly believe that they will have significant advance warning of their own death and will then be in a frame of mind to calmly plan their estates. Health care professionals, however, know that in the majority of cases death comes suddenly and unexpectedly or as a result of a sudden dramatic turn for the worse of a chronic condition.

For many people, a diagnosis of a very serious illness makes it harder, not easier, to do estate planning. In a sense, patients feel that by doing estate planning they are "giving up hope" and harming their chances of recovery. Some medical professionals believe that giving a blunt diagnosis of an impending death takes away hope and is detrimental to the patient. They are trained to encourage treatment and not give up trying to keep the patient alive. While they may not actually intend to deceive the patient, the communication they have with the patient may be received as a more optimistic view of the future than is likely to occur.

In short, it is difficult to accept one's own impending death and tempting to interpret a medical message as offering more hope for survival than it really does. It is often just too painful to think about estate planning when a person is seriously ill, because it makes the impending death feel so real. I have noticed many times, too, that people who know they are very ill simply lose interest in financial issues and want to focus their attention entirely on the people they love. This is admirable and understandable from a personal perspective, but the results are sometimes later financially devastating to the family. It is far easier emotionally to plan an estate at a time when a person is not upset by health problems and when death feels like a far distant event.

As a result of these and other factors, it is estimated that around 70 percent of Americans do no estate planning whatsoever. In almost all cases, there are negative results for the individual or the family. Some are not terribly serious, but some are devastating. Now is when "the time is right" to do your estate planning.

People sometimes worry that if they do an estate plan now, then they will be "stuck" with it and that conditions in their lives could be very different in the future. While there are some estate planning tools that are irrevocable during lifetime, they are not common. Most estate planning documents are completely revocable and amendable. Well-drafted plans can include alternatives in the documents that allow a great deal of flexibility. In short, preparing an estate plan now in no way prevents you from creating a partially or entirely different plan in the future.

Estate planning is more than just writing a will. It should encompass all aspects of financial, tax, and personal planning. People often think of estate planning only in terms of what happens after death. Long-term disability, however, is a real and common occurrence—either from illness or accident—and is often the forgotten part of estate planning.

Close to half of the population in the United States spends at least some time receiving long-term care. This fact indicates that at least half of us can anticipate some form of long-term illness or chronic disability at some time in our lives. This trend is increasing with the fact that a higher percentage of the population now lives longer. Earlier in history, many people died in young adulthood or middle age from conditions that are now successfully treated medically. The result is that our country now has an expanding group of disabled adults. Thus, each of us faces a lower likelihood of dying young but a higher likelihood of spending at least some period of our lives dependent to some degree on other people for our safety and daily needs.

This chapter will discuss estate planning needs (1) in the event of a long-term disability and (2) upon death. As difficult as these issues are to consider and plan for, they are exponentially more difficult to handle if there is no plan in place when they arise. Failure to plan for illness and death does not guarantee that these painful parts of life won't happen to us; it just guarantees that someone else will have to make these personal and serious decisions for us. It means that we relinquish our own rights to make decisions about our bodies and our property. If we are very lucky, we have family members who think just like we do on all crucial issues and everyone in the family is in complete agreement. Sadly, this is often not the case.

While none of us wants to accept the prospect of developing Alzheimer's disease or any other mentally disabling condition, the possibility is real for any one of us. Family history can give us some hint as to our future, but many of us only know about the lives of our parents and grandparents, and family lore about what happened to our ancestors may be inaccurate medically or simply incomplete. In addition, in many families our ancestors died young from conditions such as appendicitis or other serious infection, leaving us no idea what would have happened to those relatives if they had lived into old age.

In short, just because we don't know of anyone in our family who has been affected by a debilitating mental condition, we cannot be assured that we are immune from such a thing. Those people who do have a family history for these conditions are usually more aware of the risk. I am not suggesting a gloomy outlook toward our own old age, but simply advising you to recognize that a long-term disability can happen to anyone. Therefore, we are best served by planning for such a possibility rather than living in denial and throwing our future to blind fate.

In general, the most emotionally painful results come from the death or sudden illness of people who have done no planning. Family conflict can arise in ways that truly shock the family members. This is particularly common in blended families, where the current spouse is not the parent of the deceased or disabled person's adult children, but it can happen in any family. There are deeply personal and emotionally charged issues in the case of either a death or a serious disability. Decisions must be made regarding issues that the family members may neither have discussed nor in some cases even considered. Sometimes family members assume that they all share the same views on issues, but in reality they do not; they only become aware of their disagreements after a death or in a medical emergency.

Hospital workers can tell us of numerous cases where a patient is required to be discharged from the hospital because his or her health insurance will not pay for further hospitalization, and the patient is too weak or ill to return home but adamantly refuses to go to a nursing home or rehabilitation center. This is most difficult when the patient lives alone and has no in-home support. Increasingly, family members live all over the country and it may be impossible for the children or others to abruptly leave their jobs and young children and come to care for an ill parent, at least for very long.

It is also common for adult children to deny the extent to which their parent needs care from others. It is very hard for adult children to accept that parents are becoming frail and dependent—almost as hard as it is for the parents themselves to accept this reality. If the medical staff recognizes that the patient is unsafe returning home, they may be forced to ask the local government social services department to legally compel the patient to enter a rehabilitation or long-term care facility against the individual's will. Alternatively, if there is a spouse or other family members, they can be placed in the position of petitioning the court to take the decision-making authority away from the ill person. This is painful and embarrassing for everyone, not to mention expensive. Ask yourself if you really want to have a social worker or a judge who doesn't know you making decisions for you if you become very ill.

Many people spend their last months or years in a nursing home. The only obvious alternative may be to stay in the home and die early from neglect or lack of care. It is unlikely that family members or medical providers who are aware of risk to an elderly or ill person will simply accept the person's stated desire to return home and live alone if they believe the person is endangered by doing so.

If the person has the financial resources to pay for in-home care, it is much more likely that they will be able to stay in the home with hired caregivers. Legally, however, the issue is who has the legal right to make the decision about a person's living situation and finances if that person is no longer able to make safe decisions for himself or herself.

A further aspect of this issue is deciding who gets to make the decision or diagnosis that a person is no longer capable of making decisions about his or her own safety and welfare or no longer able to live safely alone. If an individual has not planned and named a legal representative, then the decision maker is likely to be a judge who takes testimony from medical providers who have examined the at-risk person. Basically, if individuals do not prepare their own estate plans, the legislature and the courts will prepare one for them.

People often have great difficulty in deciding what to do with their estates if they are married to someone who is not the parent of their children. They feel that they have to disadvantage either their spouse or children—so rather than making such a painful choice, they decline to act at all. Far too many of these cases end up in litigation or destroy the relationship between stepparents and stepchildren.

A competent and thoughtful estate planning attorney will be able to suggest alternatives to people in this situation, which will benefit both the spouse and the children and will greatly reduce the possibility of conflict after a death. This is an increasingly common issue and will be one for you if you remarry and have children from a prior marriage. You may be pleasantly surprised at the ideas your attorney can give you. You should not resist consulting an attorney just because you do not understand the options or cannot decide what to do. It is the attorney's role to educate you about the possibilities and to help you decide what you want to do. If you do not understand what your attorney tells you, ask him or her to explain it in different terms and to discuss it further until you are satisfied. An ethical attorney does not make the decisions for you or coerce you into making a particular choice.

The following sections will discuss the various basic estate planning tools that are now commonly available, what they are designed to accomplish, and some advantages and disadvantages of each. There are many other specialized or sophisticated estate planning vehicles that are not listed here, but which you can learn about in books devoted exclusively to estate planning or from your estate planning attorney if you are interested. Remember that there are three ways that assets pass to other persons upon death:

1. By will or through intestacy, using the probate process;

2. By contract, such as a beneficiary designation for assets such as life insurance, retirement plans, and IRAs or "payable on death" designations on bank accounts of all kinds and certain investment accounts; and

3. By operation of law for any asset owned in joint tenancy with another person.

## § 15.2 Wills

Wills are written documents that direct what is to happen to a person's assets upon death and that name someone to be in charge of the process. Wills can also appoint guardians for minor children. (In Colorado, children are minors until they reach age 18.) Wills might not affect what happens to everything a person owned and, in fact, only apply to the assets owned by the decedent in his or her own name or as a tenant in common with someone else. (A tenant in common is a joint owner of an asset that is not owned in joint tenancy.)

Wills can be amended or revoked during the creator's lifetime. They serve no function and have no effect during the creator's lifetime.

In Colorado, wills may be holographic (handwritten), and these are valid if written and signed entirely in the person's own handwriting. Otherwise, a will that is typed or produced on a computer must be signed by the testator/

testatrix (the person creating the will) in the presence of two independent witnesses and a notary public (who cannot also serve as a witness). A photocopy of a will is not a valid will, nor is an unsigned will.

Tangible personal property (such as furniture, cars, and jewelry) can be disposed of by using a Memorandum of Disposition of Tangible Personal Property. This is simply a list that describes items of tangible personal property and states who is to receive them upon the person's death. It must be signed and dated, and its use should be authorized in the will itself. A memorandum cannot be used to dispose of real estate, securities, insurance, or many other assets.

Wills appoint a Personal Representative (sometimes referred to as an executor or executrix) with authority to administer the estate. Wills can appoint conservators for property inherited by minors, since minors cannot take custody of inherited property. Wills can also create testamentary trusts, which are trusts that come into existence after the death of the person who created the will.

Simple will forms can be purchased from legal publishers, either in paper form or as software. They are sometimes adequate, but often do not provide optimal planning either from a tax perspective or from a family welfare point of view. I am surprised at how many such wills I encounter that have not been signed correctly and are then called into question after a death. In other cases, it is clear that the person who signed the will did not understand the meaning of parts of the document and had no one to explain them. A knowledgeable and empathetic estate planning attorney can almost always prepare a better and more appropriate will, but the cost will be greater. The future cost of a defective or inappropriate will can be enormous, however.

## § 15.3 Trusts

A trust is a written agreement by which a person (called the "grantor" or "settlor") creates a legal arrangement where a named trustee holds assets in trust for the benefit of individuals or charities (called "beneficiaries"). The most commonly used trusts in Colorado and most of the country are revocable living trusts. These trusts are created by a person during his or her lifetime and can own assets or be the beneficiary of certain assets (*e.g.*, life insurance and IRAs). They can take care of a person's assets after death and during disability. For this reason, many attorneys prefer that their clients create a revocable living trust in addition to a will. During the person's lifetime, they are usually the sole beneficiaries, and no one else obtains rights to the trust property until after death.

The trust agreement should appoint trustees and successor trustees. The grantor of the trust is usually the initial trustee, so he or she retains complete control of the trust assets while living. People often think of banks as trustees and are sometimes unwilling to create a trust if they believe that a bank must be involved; however, there is no requirement that a bank must be involved in a trust, although there are situations where this may be a good idea. Many of the trusts I encounter in Colorado name a series of individuals as trustees, sometimes naming a bank to serve as trustee if all of the individuals die or cannot act for any other reason. It is more common in some other parts of the country to see banks named as trustees. If you create a trust, this issue is completely yours to decide.

People often erroneously believe that only very wealthy people need a trust. In fact, trusts can provide significant benefits for many people. People with very little net worth may not benefit much from a trust, but I would advise you to at least explore with a good estate planning attorney whether a trust would be beneficial for you.

Trusts can protect a child's inheritance until far past his or her eighteenth birthday—even for the child's entire life, which might be desirable in some cases. Trusts can provide for a disabled beneficiary without disqualifying him or her from public benefits. They can be designed to provide for a spouse while guaranteeing that your children, rather than your current spouse's subsequent spouse, end up receiving what is left in the trust at the death of the second spouse.

There are many other kinds of trusts designed for specific purposes. If you are interested in this topic, you will likely get the best information from an attorney who focuses his or her practice on estate planning and trusts with significant knowledge about estate and gift tax.

# § 15.4 Powers of Attorney

Powers of attorney are powerful documents under Colorado law. They are used to give another person legal authority to conduct your financial affairs. The person to whom you give this authority is called an agent or attorney-in-fact. Unless you restrict the agent's powers, he or she will be able to do anything with your assets that you could do. This includes selling your home and taking all of the money out of all of your bank accounts, investment accounts, and anything else you own. Power of attorney forms are widely available both in paper form and in software packages; they can come into effect either upon signing or upon disability, and can be designed to remain in effect for the rest of your life.

Powers of attorney can avoid the need for a court petition to appoint a conservator if you become mentally disabled and can no longer manage your financial affairs. Without a power of attorney, it is likely that no one would have legal authority to manage your financial affairs if you were no longer able to do so. A family relationship does not create this kind of legal authority. If you sign a power of attorney, you can spare yourself and your family from having to go through a court process in the event of a long-term disability. You will be able to choose exactly who you would want to take care of these matters if you could not. You should name several trustworthy people, one after the other, in case your first choice dies or is unable to act for some other reason.

Powers of attorney, unfortunately, have too often been misused to deprive elderly and vulnerable people of their money and property. People often sign them at the request of a new spouse, an adult child, or a caregiver without understanding that they can be used to deprive them of everything they own. There have been many cases in Colorado where powers of attorney have been used to do just that, and the victims were not able to regain their property or money because it had all been sold or spent.

I believe that powers of attorney can be helpful and useful, but I would advise you to consult privately (without the proposed agent in the meeting) with an attorney you select yourself before signing one. You should also not appoint anyone you have not known for a significant amount of time as your agent. Consider naming at least some successor agents who are younger than you are. Agents do not have to be family members. I can think of almost no circumstances where a paid caregiver should be named as an agent under power of attorney. No one with an addiction problem or a criminal history should be appointed. A trust with a bank trustee is often a good substitute for a broad power of attorney for people who do not have trustworthy close relatives to appoint. The trust will not serve all of the same functions, but will take care of many of the problems solved with a power of attorney.

## § 15.5 Life Insurance

Life insurance passes by beneficiary designation to the people named on the beneficiary designation form in the possession of the insurance company rather than by will. Beneficiary designations are vitally important, and many people believe erroneously that changing a will automatically changes where life insurance will go. The only time a will has an effect on where life insurance goes is when all of the named beneficiaries are dead and the insurance then passes to the probate estate.

Most of the people I encounter cannot remember exactly who the beneficiary of their life insurance is. People often own life insurance for many years and never think about this issue despite dramatic changes in their families and lives. I have seen a number of cases where after a death the family discovers that an ex-spouse of the decedent is still named as beneficiary because no one thought to fill out a new form after a divorce. Widowed persons should get change of beneficiary forms from the insurance company and fill out new ones, since it is likely that the deceased spouse was the beneficiary.

Minor children should not be named as beneficiaries of life insurance. If they are, a court will have to appoint a conservator for them if the insurance becomes payable to them while they are minors. A trust for the children can be a beneficiary, or a custodian under the Uniform Transfers to Minors Act can be named. A custodian is an adult who will manage the money for the children until they are 21; no court involvement is necessary. Life insurance is an important asset, and great care should be taken with the beneficiary designation. The quality of your loved ones' lives can be dramatically affected depending on whether or not they receive life insurance.

## § 15.6 Estate Tax Issues

Estate tax is discussed in detail in Chapter 6. You should know, though, that if estate tax is an issue for you, it is possible to take many steps to minimize it through your own estate planning. You will need to consult with an attorney who has a strong expertise in estate and gift tax to help you accomplish estate tax reduction. Some estate tax planning techniques work best if they are in place for a number of years before a death, so if you want to plan to reduce estate tax for your heirs, do not delay beginning this process.

## § 15.7 Health Care Powers of Attorney

Health care powers of attorney only come into effect if you are no longer able to make your own medical treatment decisions due to your medical condition or mental disability. These documents appoint someone else, known as an agent (and ideally a list of people to serve sequentially), designated by you to make decisions about your medical care if you cannot do so. You may appoint more than one person as an agent under a health care proxy to act together. Doing so, however, can increase the chance of disagreement between the agents as to what should be done. Many people do, however, name all of their adult children to act together on medical decisions.

The decisions the agent makes are literally on life-and-death issues. Many people have strong beliefs, religious or otherwise, about end-of-life issues, including whether or not it is ever ethical to remove a person from life support or to stop artificial nourishment when a person is diagnosed as near death. If you have strong feelings on any health care issue, be sure to discuss them with the people you plan to name as your agents under a health care proxy.

Likewise, if your children have opposing ideas on these issues, you will simply be setting up a battle if you appoint all of them to act together as agents. There have been several high-profile cases in the press in the last few years involving people who were severely injured and could not eat or survive without life support and artificial nourishment. The reason that the cases received so much attention is that the patients had never named an agent under a health care proxy and they each had more than one family member with very differing ideas on how they should be treated. In all of the cases, at least one family member wanted to remove the patient from life support and at least one other relative insisted that the patient be kept alive artificially, regardless of a bleak medical diagnosis, in the hope that the condition would improve. These cases were litigated at great financial and emotional cost. If the injured people had just designated one agent to make decisions, then that person could have made the decisions and it would have been far less likely that the courts would have been involved. Agents under these documents have broad decision-making authority, including the authority to withhold treatment.

## § 15.8 Living Wills

Another document people can choose to sign is commonly referred to as a "living will." These documents have nothing to do with passing assets at death, and many people are confused by the name. Some people also confuse them with living trusts because of the name similarity. Living wills are, however, written statements by a person that if he or she is ever terminally ill and has been unconscious or comatose for a specified period of time (seven days in Colorado), then all forms of life support are to be removed. This is each person's own statement, not a decision that is delegated to anyone else. The Colorado legislature devised a form printed in our statutes, which is commonly available at hospitals. Many attorneys prepare them for their clients as well.

Living wills signed in other states or that are written differently than the Colorado statutory form may be honored here, but the Colorado form is more easily accepted since health care providers are used to seeing that form.

Since 1990, health care facilities have been required by federal law to ask new admittees if they have a living will. If they do not have one, they are asked if they want one. Many people believe that this requirement came into being as a cost-saving measure, since Medicare or Medicaid pays the cost of maintaining many people who spend considerable time on life support.

I believe that people must be free to follow their own beliefs on this most personal issue, and no one should feel pressured to agree to be removed from life support on financial grounds. I do find, however, that a significant percentage of the people I encounter do not like the idea of being kept alive artificially if there is no realistic hope of returning to a normal life. I think it is disconcerting to be asked about this issue at the time a person is being admitted to a hospital; you should consider this issue and (if you want to) sign a living will as soon as possible so that you won't have to make that decision when you are sick or injured.

It is also comforting for family members to know your wishes on this issue so they do not have to make such a difficult decision on your behalf. For many people, it is tremendously difficult emotionally to agree to disconnect a loved one from life support, even if the person is very old and has no hope of recovery. Having a signed living will gives family members knowledge about your wishes at a time when you can no longer speak for yourself.

## § 15.9 Preplanned Funerals

It is often terribly difficult for family members to plan a funeral. Mortuaries offer pre-planned (and prepaid) funeral and burial plans. The Colorado legislature has also created a statutory form that can be used to plan your funeral; to designate burial, cremation, or entombment; or to simply name another person to be in charge of the process and make the decisions. It is very comforting for families to know that they are following the wishes of their deceased family members and not to have to deal with these issues at a time when they may be grief-stricken or in shock.

I also believe that it is likely to be less expensive if we plan our own funeral and burial. Sometimes relatives who feel some guilt about their relationship with the deceased may be inclined to spend a lot of money on the funeral as a way to assuage that guilt. We are unlikely to overspend money on our own funeral. I would encourage you to preplan your funeral and burial or cremation as an act of kindness for your family.

## § 15.10 Joint Tenancy

Many people think of joint tenancy as a form of estate planning. There are problems created by joint tenancy in many situations by using this form of ownership, and I believe that it can create unforeseen problems. Joint tenancy is a form of ownership of assets between two or more people. It is often seen on deeds to real estate, particularly if owned by a married couple, but bank accounts, investments, and other assets can also be owned in joint tenancy.

In Colorado, a joint tenancy is created by titling an asset in the names of the joint owners, followed by the words "as joint tenants" or "in joint tenancy" or "as joint tenants with right of survivorship." The legal effect of joint tenancy is that if one joint tenant dies, the remaining joint tenant(s) automatically own the asset and the decedent's interest passes to them outside of probate. The simplicity of this process is its greatest advantage. You and your deceased spouse may have owned assets as joint tenants and you may have had an easy time getting control of those assets after his or her death.

Many widowed people place assets into joint tenancy with their adult children after the spouse's death. They do this for two primary reasons: (1) to avoid probate, and (2) to make it possible for someone else to access their assets if they become incapacitated. I believe that this is a mistake (for reasons I will discuss below) and that management during incapacity and probate avoidance can be managed better by using trusts.

Many people do not realize that any joint tenant who owns a bank account has the legal right to take out all of the money in the account. Also, many people do not realize that all the joint tenants must sign a deed to sell real estate. And they are not aware that if a joint tenant has creditors, the creditors can foreclose on the jointly owned property. I have seen cases where a mother placed a child's name on her accounts as a joint tenant so that he could help her pay her bills if she ever needed help; but the child had a drug addiction that his mother was unaware of and he took all of the money out of her bank accounts. She had no legal recourse to get it back and he had spent it before she knew it was gone.

In another case, a woman signed a deed placing the ownership of her home into joint tenancy with her daughter, in order to avoid probate at her death. Unbeknownst to the mother, the daughter had a large unpaid tax bill and other large debts. The daughter mortgaged the home without her mother's knowledge (yes, some lenders will do this!), spent the money, and later failed to make the mortgage payments. To the mother's horror, the bank foreclosed on her home. No probate could possibly be that expensive.

In another case, a woman signed a deed placing the ownership of her home into joint tenancy with herself and her five children. When she later wanted to sell her home and move to a warmer climate and buy a new home there, several of the children refused to sign the deed because they did not want the house sold under any circumstances, and two told her that they would only sign the deed if they were paid "their share" of the sale proceeds.

Clearly, the children in these cases were people with significant problems, and perhaps their parents were deceiving themselves about their children's honesty and capabilities. But in all of these cases, joint tenancy was not an appropriate method of planning for disability or death.

## § 15.11 Business Continuity Plans

If you own a business by yourself or with business partners, a business continuity plan is crucial. These plans are often referred to as "buy-sell" agreements and address what will happen to the interest of an owner who can no longer work due to disability or death. Without this kind of planning, a business that was built over a lifetime of work can become worthless or can tie up family members or business partners in litigation that is devastating to them financially and emotionally.

Good business continuity plans provide clear terms defining exactly what "disability" is, a method of determining the value of the business, and clear requirements as to who can or must buy out the interest of a disabled or deceased owner and how payment will be made. Life insurance is often used to fund at least part of this process.

If you are in business with at least one other person and you have not addressed these issues, I strongly urge you to work with a business attorney who can help you analyze your situation and suggest a continuity plan. If you are in business for yourself without other owners, you should clearly analyze whether or not the business could continue successfully without you, if there are key employees or identifiable third parties who would be interested in buying the business if you died or could no longer work, or if the business would simply close. Often, a good business attorney can help you create a plan that would recognize value for your family even if you were no longer working in the business and make a plan of action for preserving the value of the business.

## § 15.12 Beneficiary Deeds

In 2004, the Colorado legislature passed a law authorizing so-called "beneficiary deeds." Under current and prior law, people can give real estate to other people as a current gift by signing a deed transferring title to the property and recording it in the county clerk and recorder's office. The person receiving the property by deed becomes the current owner of the real estate. Beneficiary deeds, in contrast, are deeds signed and recorded during lifetime, but which do not pass ownership until the person giving the deed (the grantor) dies. They are designed to avoid probate for the property involved.

There are specific forms that must be used for beneficiary deeds, or the person making the transfer will inadvertently transfer the property during his or her lifetime. The beneficiary deed must be recorded during the grantor's lifetime to be effective. The grantor can revoke the transfer by recording a later deed. The person receiving the property under the beneficiary deed does not have any rights to the property until the grantor dies. These deeds appear to be designed to avoid probate the way joint tenancy does, without some of the risks of joint tenancy.

# CHAPTER 16
# RE-ENTERING LIFE

## § 16.1 Returning to Work—When Is "Too Soon"?

If you were working before your spouse's death, you should avoid making a sudden decision to retire or resign from your job. You may not need to work for financial reasons, but as in so many other decisions after the death of a spouse, you should take some considerable time to think about this decision. You may actually need to work because you need the money, but you may not realize this for several months while you sort through your finances and understand how they have changed as a result of your spouse's death. In most cases, household income goes down after the death of one spouse, but this may not be immediately obvious to you.

Your work may be an important part of your identity and may give great meaning to your life. As with any decision to retire, it is vitally important to ask yourself what you will be doing with your time if you are not working, particularly if you are now alone at home. Work adds structure to time, and many widowed people find comfort in a routine so that they do not have to constantly be thinking about how to fill their days.

You should not return to work so soon that you cannot function on the job because of acute emotional distress. You should also not plan to stay away from your job until you feel "normal" again, since this will likely take many months.

A significant practical reality is that employers will not hold a position empty indefinitely. It is probably practical to expect to return to work after a couple of weeks or so. You may not want to volunteer for any enormously stressful projects for a while if you can avoid it.

## § 16.2 Resuming a Social Life

Your social life as a widowed person will be different than it was when you were married. If much of your socializing centered around your spouse and his or her friends and activities, it will change a great deal. As unfair as it seems, you will probably have to make more effort than you did when married to have a satisfying social life.

If you have regularly scheduled social activities, such as golf or tennis leagues, book clubs, bridge groups, and the like, by all means continue them. These are often not "couples" activities and are things you enjoy doing as an individual that do not depend on participation by a spouse.

If people invite you to parties, dinners, and other social occasions, make an effort to attend even if you do not feel enthusiastic about it. It can be unhealthy to stay home alone all the time and you might enjoy the event more than you anticipate.

## § 16.2.1 Your Spouse's Family and Friends

Many widowed people find that their deceased spouse's family and friends drift out of contact within a few months of the death. If your spouse was the person who made most of the social plans during your marriage, you may now have to begin to make the effort to keep in contact with your spouse's relatives, friends, and business acquaintances—even if this is not a comfortable process for you—if you want to maintain those relationships.

I do not believe that people intentionally abandon widowed spouses of friends or relatives, but often the decedent was the point of contact or the person who took it upon himself or herself to make plans to get together. If the person who did all the planning is not around to do it anymore, it will not happen unless someone else makes the effort.

You may not be terribly interested in maintaining relationships with your spouse's family or friends. If you have young children, though, it can be a true loss in their lives to lose contact with their deceased parent's family. If your spouse's family is not good at staying in contact with you or your children, please consider making the effort to keep your children in the lives of your spouse's family.

If your relationships as a married couple revolved around a particular interest of your late spouse's that you do not share, it is likely that you will drift apart from the people you knew in that sphere unless you make the effort to keep in contact. Some widowed people feel that they are excluded from "couples" gatherings. While some social occasions might seem more appropriate for couples, I encourage friends and family to remember to include widowed people in social events. There are very few kinds of gatherings that cannot include single people. Do not worry about having an even number of single men and women. As a host or hostess you are planning a fun event, not match-making, so be inclusive.

Alternatively, you must decide if you really want to continue a relationship with certain friends or relatives of your spouse. If we are honest with ourselves, it is likely that at least some of our spouse's friends or family members are people we do not have much in common with or who we merely accepted during the marriage because our spouse was fond of them. You can now decide to let marginal relationships simply fade away if you choose.

## § 16.2.2 Maintaining Friendships

The friendships you have with people who share your individual interests and that were not based on "couple" relationships should continue as before, provided that you continue to participate in the same activities that you did when your spouse was living. If you want to maintain friendships with people you always saw as a couple, you probably are going to have to make a conscious effort to get together with those people by planning events and social occasions. I have noticed that some widowed people expect other people to always do the planning and inviting, and after a while, when they do not reciprocate other people's invitations, the invitations from others stop and they become isolated and lonely.

You will have a big rush of attention right after your spouse's death, but soon everyone will get back to their own busy lives. Some people will feel uncomfortable around you because they know how sad you are or are afraid they will not know what to talk about with you. It will help to make an effort to talk about "normal" things when you are with friends, so people understand that you can still participate in life. Some widowed people believe that people are avoiding them on purpose, when the truth is that the deceased spouse was the catalyst for the relationship and without him or her, the bond is not very strong.

## § 16.2.3 Taking Up New Activities and Making New Friends

If your social life was based primarily on your spouse's interests, it will now be important for you to participate in activities that you enjoy and that will let you make new friends who know you as a single person. This can involve joining a religious congregation (if that is appealing to you) and participating in the group's activities that go beyond weekly services. It can mean volunteering for a socially beneficial cause. One way to stop focusing on our own loss is to work for the benefit of other people.

You might consider learning to play bridge or other card games and joining a group that plays regularly. You could take up golf and play with a regular group. You could reconnect with an alumni group or a sorority or fraternity alumni group, lodge, veterans group, choir or musical group, bowling league, quilting or needlework group, or other special-interest organization.

Many universities have programs where people over the age of 65 can audit classes without charge. Other institutions offer adult classes on various non-academic but enjoyable topics (*e.g.,* photography, painting, and woodworking). You could choose to enroll in an academic program for credit and earn an advanced degree or earn your high school diploma or bachelor's degree if you did not have one before. You might be interested in politics and become involved in a campaign or party volunteerism. You could join a health club and participate in fitness classes. Some people work on fundraising committees and plan benefits to support worthy causes. If you have an interest in travel, you might join tour groups. Some universities plan guided trips for their alumni, which can be enjoyable because the participants have the bond of having gone to the same school. It can be difficult to make yourself get started, but if you can participate in a few regularly scheduled activities that you enjoy, it will keep you from being so isolated and propel you into new social contacts. It is easier to have recurring activities than to always have to think of what to do for a day or an evening.

When you are ready to start resuming social activities, it may be easiest to start attending movies, sporting events, plays, concerts, and the like and inviting a friend to join you. You might get two season tickets to a concert series or baseball games and make a point of inviting someone to join you at each event.

Soon, though, you need to start entertaining again, particularly if you want other people to continue to reciprocate and invite you to their gatherings. A "couples" dinner party may not be comfortable anymore, but you can always give cocktail parties, buffet dinners, barbecues, and brunches where people mix and mingle rather than having assigned seats with an absolutely equal balance of men and women. You can be the person who plans parties to celebrate other people's happy occasions, such as a friend's child's engagement or someone's birthday. You can plan parties around sporting events or outdoor activities. If you are a man and your late wife always planned the parties, you could ask a friend who is an experienced host or hostess to co-host a gathering with you and show you how to plan a party. You can focus on very simple gatherings featuring pizza and watching sports events on television, or you can hire a caterer. One way to be sure you have a social life is to create it yourself. This may not be easy or natural for you, but you should make the attempt.

## § 16.3 Those "First" Holidays and Anniversaries

Holidays have a lot of emotional "baggage" for many people under the best of circumstances. Some widowed people simply cannot face the idea of a holiday at home during the first year and make plans to take a trip and do something completely different than they ever did before on that date. If you are in an exotic foreign country, you will not be terribly conscious of the fact that it is Thanksgiving. Some people, if they can afford it, start taking their children and grandchildren on cruises or beach vacations instead of having traditional holiday celebrations at home.

Some people take a trip to visit out-of-town friends or relatives and celebrate with them. Other people create new holiday traditions for themselves that are quite different than what they did when married. You could perhaps start giving an annual Christmas Eve open house rather than the family-only formal dinner you used to serve. Some people focus on the less fortunate at holidays and work in homeless shelters or soup kitchens or help charitable groups with their activities. If you have young children, they will likely want to do what you have always done on the holiday. It might be less difficult if you invite some new people to your gathering so the group gets larger rather than smaller. There always seem to be people who do not have family nearby who would welcome an invitation to celebrate with another family.

## § 16.4 Dating

It will probably take some time to think of yourself as a single person again. You may feel married even though you are not anymore. You do not have to ever develop a romantic relationship again, but you may want to. It may have been many years since you dated, so if you want to start dating again, it is probably most comfortable to begin seeing someone you have known for some time. Some widowed people begin dating within a few months after the death of a spouse, which adult children or other family members sometimes consider to be disrespectful to the memory of the deceased spouse. You have the right to follow your own feelings in this area, though, and your choice to begin dating is no one else's decision to make.

Be aware, though, that sometimes family and friends are simply concerned that you may not be thinking clearly yet and that you could be easily manipulated by someone who wants to exploit you for his or her own financial gain. As much as we do not like to think about it, there are people who prey on the newly widowed and exploit their emotional vulnerability for their own financial gain. I have seen unfortunate situations where new "friends" of either gender start an intense and romantic courtship of a widowed person and try to take over the finances to "help" the widowed person. It is very flattering to have someone be so interested in us, but be very wary of anyone who asks to get involved in your finances or asks you to change your estate planning for his or her benefit. Also be cautious about anyone who wants to rush into marriage. You are both adults and there is no need to make such an important decision in haste.

I have also noticed that some people with serious personal problems, like drug addiction, alcoholism, and various personality disorders, seem to always want to be in relationships and pursue romances with people they see as lonely and vulnerable. If you meet someone new, take your time and really get to know the person and his or her family and friends before committing to anything. Be wary of people without friends and family or who move frequently, change jobs frequently, or have a lot of instability of any kind in their lives. You will not be able to change them, and they can cause you a great deal of pain.

Young children might be upset when a widowed parent begins to date. It is probably best not to involve a new romantic partner in your family life unless and until the relationship becomes serious. Children who have lost a parent do not need to have other adults entering and leaving their lives repeatedly. If a relationship is becoming serious, introduce the new person in a casual setting and take things very gradually. Remember that the people you bring into your own life will also come to influence your children, and you have an obligation to make certain that the adults you expose your children to are positive influences on them. If your children are adults, you still need to be selective about your romantic partners for your own sake, but at least you will not be harming young children if you make a bad choice of companion.

## § 16.5 Remarriage

Many widowed people do remarry. A large percentage of our widowed male clients remarry within a couple of years unless they are in very poor health or are quite elderly. Many women also remarry, but in my experience, not usually as soon as the men do. I have observed that many widowed people remarry another widowed person (or a divorced person) who was part of their social group during their marriage.

People of all ages marry for all kinds of reasons. Widowed people, though, can be particularly vulnerable to making mistakes in remarrying very quickly after a death. If you feel that you are desperate to remarry because you cannot stand to be alone, you risk making an inappropriate choice that will cause you pain. Think of how painful it would be to face a divorce after losing a spouse to death. As with most other decisions you make after the death of a spouse, there is no need to rush into a marriage.

Children are often concerned about a widowed parent's decision to remarry, for two primary reasons. The first is that they may not like the new spouse or fear that he or she will disrupt their family relationships. The second is that they fear that the new spouse will exploit the parent's finances or that the parent will change their estate plan and leave everything to the new spouse. These are legitimate concerns in some cases. In others, they are simply selfish.

Unfortunately, there have been many cases where people who were dishonest, unstable, or manipulative have swept vulnerable widowed people of both genders off their feet and into a hasty marriage, only to victimize them financially and emotionally in the new marriage. There are many warning signals you should pay attention to, but consider the following as danger signs for a new marriage:

- The new person is in a big hurry to get married. This is a particularly bad sign if he or she has been recently divorced.

- The new person will not tell you much about his or her past.

- The new person does not have a job (if younger than retirement age), group of friends, or ties to the community.

- The new person does not introduce you to his or her family.

- The new person has a history of domestic violence or any kind of violence or fraud. It is particularly dangerous if the new person blames past victims for his or her own violent and abusive behavior and does not take responsibility for his or her own actions.

- The new person hits you, your children, or your pets.

- The new person asks you for money or seems to be drowning in debt.

- The new person asks for information about your finances and/or wants to "help" you invest your money or deal with your finances (always use a qualified professional!).

- The new person asks you to sign a power of attorney giving him or her access to your money and property or asks you to put his or her name as joint owner with you of your assets.

- The new person asks you to change your will in his or her favor.

- The new person appears to want you to feel sorry for him or her.

- The new person abuses drugs or alcohol, or other people who are trustworthy tell you that he or she does so when not with you.

- People you trust are concerned that the new person may have serious character flaws that could hurt you.

- The new person has been divorced in the past and places all the blame for the failure of the marriage on his or her former spouse without thoughtfully taking some personal responsibility.

- The new person does not pay court-ordered child support or spend time with his or her children from a prior relationship.

- You discover discrepancies in the information the new person gives you or evidence that he or she is lying to you about anything.

If you find yourself attracted to someone who exhibits any of these (or other) negative traits or behaviors, consider getting some counseling from a reliable professional to help you understand your motivation and the possible consequences to your life of a serious involvement with such a person. If you are simply very lonely, ask for help in forming a plan to fill your life with more people and activities that will not be so risky for your future. Also explore the traits you find attractive and admirable in other people so you can be conscious about your choices in companions and any future spouse. Above all else, do not rush into a marriage. While living together before marriage violates some people's religious principles, it can give you an insight into what lies ahead in a contemplated marriage. It is harder to hide negative behavior from someone you live with than from someone you do not live with.

It is becoming more common for people contemplating a serious relationship or marriage to hire a private investigator to check public records about a new person in their lives. This is probably unnecessary if you have known the person for years, but it might be wise if he or she is new in your life. I have known of a number of cases where very surprising negative information about a potential new spouse was revealed by a private investigator. This includes records that the person is currently married to someone else or has had multiple undisclosed divorces, bankruptcies, tax liens, criminal convictions, claims for unpaid child support (even for undisclosed children), and in a few cases, records showing that the person is married to more than one other person at the same time. As disappointing as it might be to discover negative information, it would be far more devastating emotionally to discover it after a marriage and to be placed in the position of needing to consider divorce.

If you have young children or teenagers living with you, it is particularly important to be careful about the person you marry since he or she will become an important influence on your children, for good or ill. I highly recommend that you, your children, and your proposed new spouse take advantage of the programs and private counselors who can help new stepfamilies work through the issues they face prior to a remarriage.

Second or subsequent marriages where there are minor children living in the home have a high failure rate. Do not underestimate the challenges facing stepfamilies, but take positive steps to address them in advance. It is crucial that all of you communicate honestly about your thoughts and feelings about the new marriage. This likely will require that you learn to listen calmly to statements that you may not like from your children. It is essential that the children are encouraged to keep communicating honestly and for them to know that they will be safe doing so. The adults must also be committed to communicating with each other and the children in an honest but mature fashion and refraining from destructive statements or hostility.

## § 16.5.1 Finances, Estate Planning, and Remarriage— Protecting Yourself and Your Children

If you do remarry, it is crucially important for you and your new spouse to thoroughly discuss how you will structure your financial lives after the marriage. In general, I recommend that you keep your assets separate, at least for the first few years, and that both of you decide how much each of you will contribute to the joint household expenses.

I highly recommend that anyone who has children and enters into a second or subsequent marriage consult with an attorney who works with premarital agreements and seriously consider requesting that your new spouse sign one.

I would also recommend that you consult with an estate planning attorney about the changes the new marriage can bring to your estate plan. I would not rush into making wholesale revisions. You should understand, however, that marriage gives your new spouse some important legal rights to your estate, which you may want to address in a premarital agreement. Some people marry a widowed person and expect him or her to change their estate plan and leave everything to the new spouse. In my experience, most mature people do not want to completely disinherit their children upon remarriage. A good estate planning attorney can advise you on ways to meet your goals. This issue needs to be addressed prior to the new marriage.

## § 16.5.2 Premarital Agreements

By using a premarital agreement, you and a new spouse can agree to waive or vary certain legal rights of spouses on divorce or death or both. A couple can agree that they will each keep the assets they own prior to the marriage separate during the marriage and that those assets will not be subject to division upon a divorce. The couple can agree to waive marital support. The court retains the authority to order support for children and to deal with custody issues. The couple can agree to waive the rights they are given by law to inherit a certain percentage of a spouse's estate. This does not prohibit the spouses from leaving bequests to each other, but is an agreement that they will not sue each other's estates. They can waive their rights to serve as Personal Representative of each other's estates, as well as guardian or conservator if either becomes disabled.

In my experience, most of the mature clients who consult me on this issue enter into premarital agreements where both spouses waive all rights to each other's property on divorce, maintenance (formerly called alimony), and all rights to inherit. In some cases, if the marriage goes well, the spouses later decide to leave each other part of their estates. But in general, they leave the bulk of their estates to their children by prior marriages.

Some couples choose not to agree to waive their inheritance rights, but only to deal with divorce issues. An agreement can be customized to meet your desires. Some family law attorneys and estate planning attorneys work in the area of these agreements.

Asking a future spouse to enter into a premarital agreement takes tact and sensitivity, and is sometimes perceived as an expression of lack of faith in the marriage. These agreements do offer significant legal protection, though, and I suggest you seriously consider one prior to a new marriage if you have any assets and have children by a prior marriage. Premarital agreements can be revoked or amended in the future by mutual agreement of the parties.

To be valid, the agreement needs to be entered into voluntarily and with full disclosure by both parties as to their assets and liabilities. Each party should have a separate attorney. The agreement should not be signed right before the marriage, and the issue of a premarital agreement should be dealt with well before the date of a marriage.

## § 16.6 When it Is Unsafe or Unhealthy to Live Alone

In some cases, due to age or health concerns—and despite my general advice not to make a decision to move soon after the death of a spouse—for some widowed people it is simply unsafe to continue to live in an environment where they will be alone. If you were dependent on your spouse to take care of you in important ways and now are unable to provide for your own basic needs, you may need to face the uncomfortable reality that you need to move to an environment where other people can provide the care you need.

Some people's health prevents them from providing for their own meals, transportation, laundry, home maintenance, and other essential functions of life. I have seen situations where an elderly widowed person became malnourished and very ill due to the inability to care for himself or herself and cases where a home quickly became a fire and health hazard because the owner was unable to clean and maintain it.

Sometimes adult children raise these issues with newly widowed parents and the parent is upset by the implication that he or she can no longer live independently. If your children are discussing this with you, listen to their concerns with an open mind and work together to make a plan for your care and safety that keeps you as independent as possible but also keeps you safe.

## § 16.7 Summary

Life does go on after the death of a spouse. It is both a continuation of a previous life and yet different in essential ways. You did not choose what happened to your life as a result of the death of your spouse, but you can choose to take control of the many facets of your life and deliberately shape a future that will in time offer you joy again.

# Glossary

**Abatement** – If the estate is not sufficient to pay all of the bequests in a will, the distributions will be reduced proportionately among the beneficiaries. This is referred to as abatement.

**Accounting** – Records that begin with the assets of the decedent on the date of death and show the income, gain, loss, and expenses paid by the estate, and the distributions to the beneficiaries. Accountings are often kept according to approved probate format.

**Ademption** – If the will specified that a certain asset was to pass to a certain beneficiary but the asset no longer was owned by the decedent at death, the bequest lapses and is referred to as having been adeemed.

**Adjusted Gross Estate** – An estate tax concept indicating the value of everything the decedent owned or had economic rights in, reduced by debts and claims.

**Alternate Valuation Date** – The date six months after the date of death, which may be used to value the estate for estate tax purposes if the estate tax will be reduced by doing so.

**Ancillary Probate** – A probate proceeding in a state other than the state where the decedent was domiciled. Usually required because the decedent owned real estate in a state other than the state of domicile.

**Annual Exclusion Amount** – Currently, individuals can make gifts of most kinds of assets if valued at $11,000 or less each year to as many people as he or she would like, free of transfer tax. For example, a grandmother could give each of her five grandchildren shares of stock worth $11,000 each without any gift tax or other tax imposed on the gift.

**Applicable Exclusion Amount** – The amount of value a decedent can pass to persons other than a surviving spouse or charity without incurring estate tax. In 2005, the aggregate amount is $1,500,000. Under current law, this amount is scheduled to increase to $2,000,000 on January 1, 2006 and to $3,500,000 on January 1, 2009.

**Basis** – The cost of an asset increased by improvements made to the asset and reduced by depreciation claimed on the asset. Basis is used to calculate how much capital gain tax will be due on the sale of an asset that has increased in value. Assets owned by a decedent receive a new basis of the date-of-death value of the asset. This is referred to as a "stepped-up basis."

**Beneficiary** – A person who is designated to receive benefits from a trust or will.

**Bequest** – A distribution provided for in a will or a trust.

**Bond** – The guaranty of a third-party financial institution for the performance of the duty of a fiduciary.

**Bypass Trust** – A frequently used trust arrangement designed to hold the Applicable Exclusion Amount for the beneficiaries while keeping the assets separate from the taxable estate of the surviving spouse.

**Conservator** – A fiduciary appointed by a court to be responsible for the assets of a disabled or minor person. Disability refers to mental incapacity to manage financial matters.

**Cost Basis** – See Basis.

**Court** – The legal forum with authority to transfer assets of a decedent to the persons entitled to receive them by will or intestacy. In Colorado, the state district courts for the various counties have jurisdiction over probate matters, except for the City and County of Denver, which has the state's only fully dedicated probate court and probate judge and magistrate.

**Credit Shelter Trust** – See Bypass Trust (these are alternative terms for the same legal arrangement).

**Death Certificate** – An official document issued by a government agency giving information about the decedent, including cause of death. State-certified death certificates are needed to transfer ownership of many assets and to make claims for assets such as life insurance and retirement plans.

**Derivatives** – Derivatives are an investment and can be any of several kinds of contracts that are valued based on the performance of other assets, such as stock in a corporation. They are typically used by large institutional investors and can be quite risky.

**Designated Beneficiary** – The person named on a beneficiary form to receive benefits from retirement plans and life insurance. The designation must be in writing and will supersede a contrary designation in a will.

**Devise** – The bequest of real property in a will.

**Disclaimer** – The process of declining to receive an asset from a decedent, under a will, trust, beneficiary designation, or joint tenancy. A disclaimer must be filed with the proper person, institution, or court no later than nine months after the date of death.

**Domicile** – The state of legal residence of a decedent. Each decedent can have only one domicile. Domicile determines which state law governs the administration of an estate.

**Elections** – Any of a number of choices that can be made on estate tax returns. These choices are made on the return or attached to it.

**Elective Share** – Many states have laws providing that a surviving spouse can take an elective share of a certain percentage of the value of the estate of a deceased spouse instead of accepting the bequests in a will.

**Estate** – The assets owned by a decedent at death. There are different kinds of estates, such as taxable estates and probate estates, which can be quite different.

**Estate Tax Return** – A federal form 706, which must be filed for the estate of a decedent whose gross estate exceeds the Applicable Exclusion Amount. Some estates that must file returns are not required to pay tax. Some states have their own estate tax systems requiring a different return to be filed and perhaps a tax to be paid. Colorado currently does not have an estate or inheritance tax.

**Executor/Executrix** – The person in charge of the administration of a probate estate, called the Personal Representative in some states (including Colorado).

**Final Income Tax Return** – A final federal and state income tax return must be filed for a decedent for the part of the year that he or she was living. The return should be clearly marked as a final return.

**General Power of Appointment** – A power given to a person in a will or trust to direct where certain assets will go without restriction.

**Generation-Skipping Transfer Tax** – A tax on assets passing to beneficiaries who are more than one generation younger than a decedent. This tax is in addition to estate or inheritance tax. It is currently 48 percent of the value of assets exceeding $1,500,000 passing to so-called "skip" persons, who are often grandchildren.

**Gross Estate** – The value of all assets of a decedent, not reduced by any liabilities.

**Guardian** – The person appointed by the court to be responsible for a minor or disabled person and to make all decisions about the protected person's living situation and medical treatment. In Colorado, people can designate guardians for their minor children in wills or other documents, but a guardianship for an adult requires a court proceeding.

**Guardian Ad Litem** – A person appointed by the court to protect the rights of a minor or disabled person. This person may or may not be an attorney and has responsibility to report to the court and make recommendations to the judge.

**Heir** – A person designated by law to inherit from a decedent.

**Holographic Will** – A will that is wholly handwritten and signed by a decedent.

**Income in Respect of a Decedent** – Income earned by the decedent but not received until after his or her death.

**Inheritance Tax** – A tax imposed on the beneficiaries based on the value of the assets they inherit. Colorado does not currently have an inheritance tax, although other states do.

**Inter Vivos Trust** – A trust created by a person during lifetime. Also called a living trust.

**Intestacy** – A person is intestate if he or she died without a will. In this case, state law dictates who will inherit and who has priority for appointment as Personal Representative.

**Inventory** – An accurate list of the decedent's assets with their fair market value on the date of death.

**IRA** – Individual retirement account authorized and regulated under federal law to provide tax-deferred growth of retirement funds.

**Irrevocable** – A document, usually a trust or will, which cannot be changed after signing.

**Irrevocable Life Insurance Trust** – A trust that owns and is the beneficiary of life insurance.

**IRS** – Internal Revenue Service.

**Joint Tenancy** – A form of property ownership between two or more owners, which automatically passes ownership to the surviving joint tenant(s) if one of them dies.

**Lapse** – If a bequest cannot be made, it is referred to as having lapsed.

**Letters of Administration** – The court-approved document showing the authority of a Personal Representative of an intestate estate.

**Letters Testamentary** – The court-approved document showing the authority of a Personal Representative of a testate estate (i.e., one where there was a will).

**Living Trust** – A trust created during a person's lifetime.

**Living Will** – An end-of-life document authorizing removal of life support and medical treatment.

**Marital Deduction** – The federal estate tax unlimited deduction that allows spouses to inherit an unlimited amount of value from a deceased spouse without paying federal estate tax.

**Personal Property** – Furniture, household contents, vehicles, art, other movable items.

**Personal Representative** – The person appointed by the court to supervise the administration of a probate estate.

**POD Designation** – A designation that can be added to bank accounts and certain other kinds of accounts instructing the financial institution to "pay on death" the account to a specified person or trust.

**Pour-over Will** – A will that directs that all probate assets be added to the assets of a separate trust, to be administered according to the terms of the trust.

**Power of Appointment** – Authority given in a will or trust to direct to whom certain property will pass.

**Probate** – The court process of transferring title to the assets of a decedent according to the will or the laws of intestacy. Probate can be formal or informal, supervised or unsupervised. The great majority of Colorado probate cases do not require court appearances.

**Probate Asset** – An asset owned by a decedent alone, without a joint owner or beneficiary designation, which will require the probate process to effect valid title transfer to the beneficiaries.

**Probate Court** – The court division responsible for handling probate matters.

**Qualified Domestic Trust** – A special trust designed to qualify bequests to non-U.S. citizen spouses for the unlimited marital deduction from federal estate tax.

**Qualified Plan** – Any one of several kinds of tax-deferred retirement plans authorized and governed by federal law.

**Qualified Terminable Interest Trust** – A special kind of marital trust often used in second marriages to provide for a surviving spouse but to ensure that the assets remaining in the trust at the second spouse's death pass to the children of a prior marriage.

**Real Property** – Land and buildings.

**Receipt and Release** – A form typically requested from beneficiaries acknowledging that they have received what they are entitled to under an estate or trust.

**Residuary** – The part of the estate that passes after payment of all taxes, debts, expenses, and specific bequests.

**Revocable Living Trust** – A trust created during a person's lifetime, which the creator can amend and revoke at will during his or her lifetime.

**Small Estate Proceeding** – A simplified form of administration for small estates where the decedent did not own real property in his or her sole name.

**Spousal Right of Election** – The right of a surviving spouse to "elect against a will" and receive a certain percentage of the augmented estate in lieu of receiving a bequest under a will or trust. Requires a court action.

**Tax Allocation** – Language in a will or trust (or without this, by state law) determining the source of payment of taxes owed by an estate.

**Tax Cost Basis** – The original cost of an asset, increased by improvements, and decreased by depreciation. Tax cost basis is used to determine how much capital gain tax is owed when a capital asset is sold. On death, assets receive a new tax cost basis of date-of-death value.

**Taxable Estate** – The assets of a decedent that are required to be included in the estate for tax purposes. Can be much broader than a probate estate and include far more value.

**Testator** – A man who executes a will. A woman who executes a will is called a testatrix.

**Trust** – A legal arrangement where a person transfers ownership of assets to a trustee for management on behalf of beneficiaries. There are many kinds of trusts used for various purposes.

**Trustee** – The person who manages trust property.

**Will** – A written document created and signed during a person's lifetime directing to whom his or her property will pass at death. Wills also appoint a Personal Representative to administer the estate and can appoint guardians and conservators for minor children.

# APPENDIX
## Grief Support Resources

| | | | |
|---|---|---|---|
| Grief | Bear Valley Church 10001 W. Jewell, Lakewood | 303-975-4000 | Support Group |
| Grief | Boulder Center for Grief & Loss Longmont & Boulder | 303-442-0248 | Healing Circles for kids. Groups for ages 6-11 and 12-18 in Longmont & Boulder. |
| Grief | Camp Comfort – part of Mt. Evans Hospice, Evergreen | 303-674-6400 | Weekend camp held in Granby, CO for children ages 6-12 dealing with loss and grief. |
| Grief | Caring Connections Ed. Center 5650 Greenwood Plaza Blvd., Greenwood Village | 303-721-6955 | Counseling and support groups – children and adults. |
| Grief | Christian Care Counseling 2600 S. Parker, Bldg 6, #263, Aurora | 303-751-1700 | Children traumatized by accident, death, etc. |
| Grief | Exempla Lutheran Hospital | 303-467-4979 | Bereavement support groups for adults. |
| Grief | Footprints St. Mary's Church, 6853 S. Prince, Littleton | 303-798-8506 | Grief support group. |
| Grief | Hospice of Boulder County | 303-449-7740 | Free groups – children, teens, parents, pregnancy, widows, suicide (Heartbeat), homicide, infant loss – family camp in August. |

| Grief | Hospice of Metro Denver 425 S. Cherry, Denver | 303-321-2828 | Ongoing children/teen groups (ages 3-18), time limited children/teen group, parent support groups, and other grief support groups. |
|---|---|---|---|
| Grief | Judi's House 1600 St. Paul (big four-story house with many activities/ centers for kids) | 720-941-0331 | Free support groups for children ages 3-18 who have experienced the death of a loved one. Groups for ages 3-5, 6-10, 11-14, 15-18. Parents/caregivers may also meet voluntarily at same time. |
| Grief | Lutheran Medical Center 8300 W. 38th Ave., Wheat Ridge | 303-425-2229 | Parent partners – match/volunteers – pregnancy or newborn loss – SOLACE – pregnancy or newborn loss grief support groups – for children ages 6-18, for adults, peer support suicide. |
| Grief | Peg Nelson Brighton, Ft. Collins | 303-912-9770 | Counselor. Does lots of grief work, including loss of a child. |
| Grief | St. Vrain Valley Parenting Center 803 3rd Ave., Longmont | 303-776-5348 | Grief counseling for kids and teens. |
| Grief | Tabor Funeral Home & Rice Mortuary 75 S. 13th Ave., Brighton | 303-654-0112 | Offer free 10-week grief support class for those suffering from the death of a loved one. Given by Peg Nelson. |

| Grief | Widowed Persons Service 1420 S. Holly | 303-764-5996 | Several groups in metro area. Friendship group, 2nd Sat. of month at Calvary Presby Church – 2:00 p.m. FREE. |
|---|---|---|---|
| Grief – Children | Rainbows 6325 S. University, Littleton | 303-794-2683 | Small support groups for kids (ages 5-18). |
| Grief – Support | Caring Friends 1656 S. Van Dyke Way, Lakewood | 303-989-5960 | Continuous support group for young widows and widowers 20-45 and their children. |
| Grief – Suicide Support | Heartbeat Narice Tom & Jackie Bob, Jan, Cheryl in Boulder | 303-934-8464 303-424-4094 303-770-1859 303-444-3496 | Support groups for adult suicide survivors. |
| Grief – Support | Community Education & Bereavement – Recovering Balance After Death Kim at Boulder Hospice | 303-415-3410 | Programs for families and children who have lost a loved one. Camp in Sept. |
| Grief – Support for Kids | Lutheran Hospice Care – Grief Relief for Kids 8300 W. 38th Ave., Wheat Ridge | 303-425-8000 | |

# Index

## V

## W